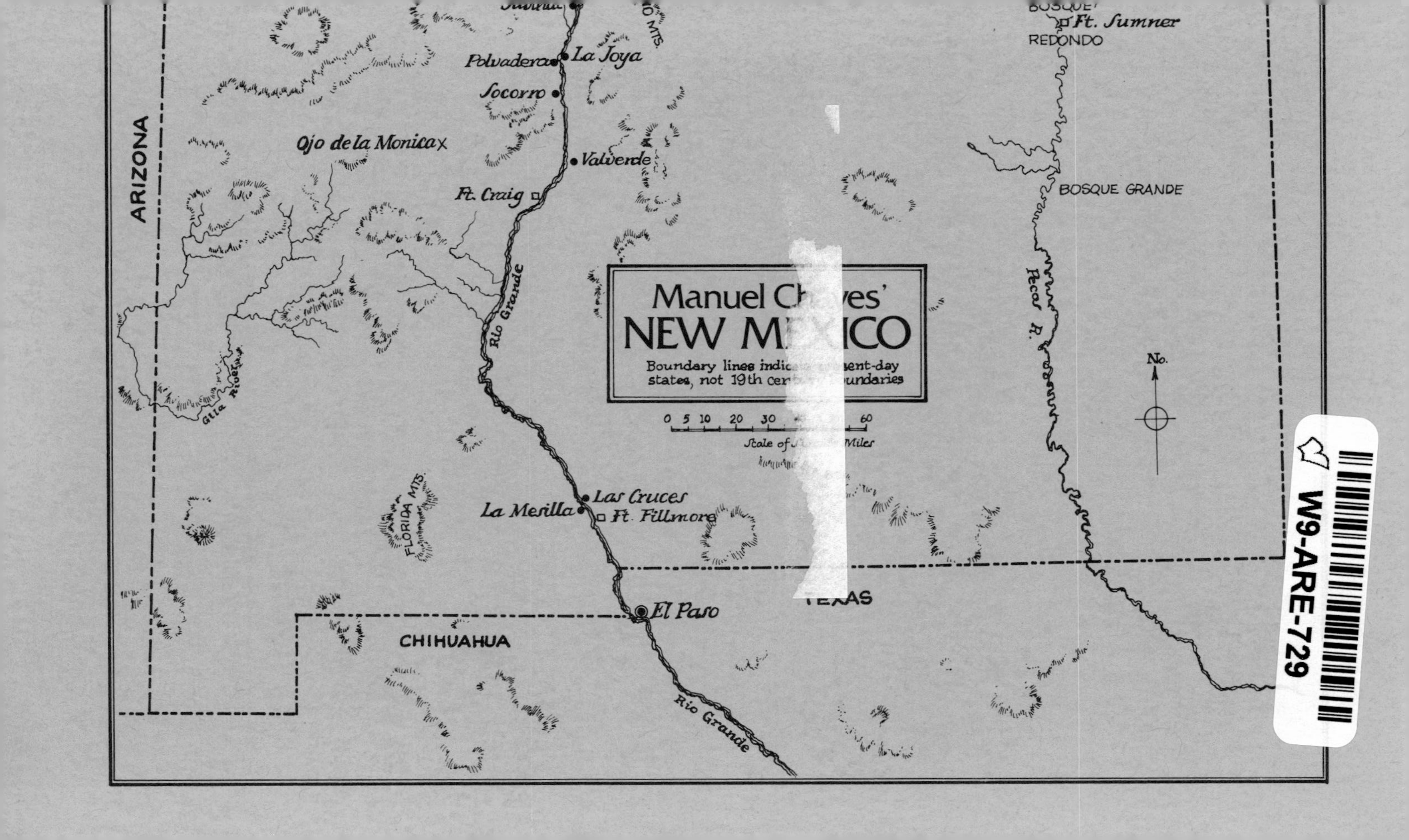

NEW MEXICO
Boundary lines indic
sent-day
states, not 19th cent
oundaries
0 5 10 20 30 60
Scale of
Miles
Ft. Sumner
REDONDO
BOSQUE GRANDE
Pecos R.
No.
Polvadera
La Joya
Socorro
Ojo de la Monica
Valverde
Ft. Craig
ARIZONA
Rio Grande
Gila River
FLORIDA MTS.
Las Cruces
La Mesilla
Ft. Fillmore
El Paso
TEXAS
CHIHUAHUA
Rio Grande

the LITTLE LION of the SOUTHWEST

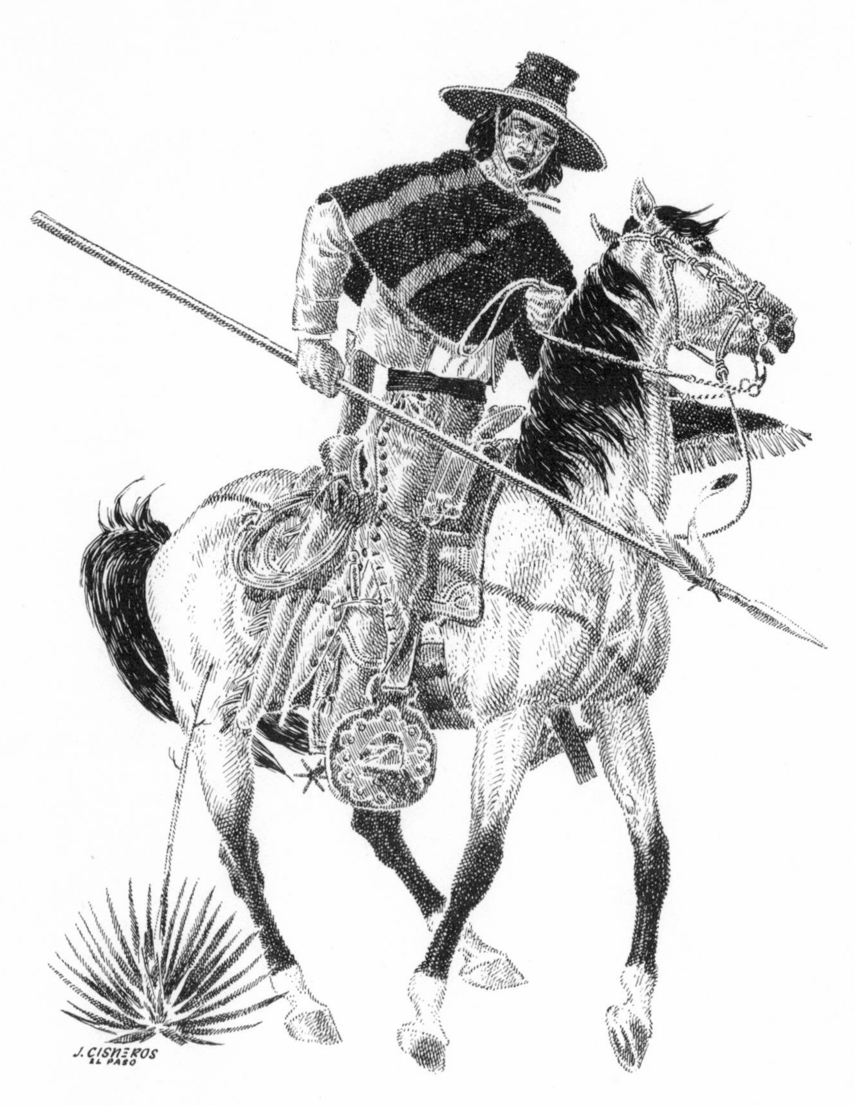

Early 19th Century New Mexican Indian Fighter

the LITTLE LION of the SOUTHWEST

a life of Manuel Antonio Chaves

MARC SIMMONS

SAGE BOOKS

THE SWALLOW PRESS INC.
CHICAGO

Printed in the United States of America

First Edition
First Printing

Sage Books are published by
The Swallow Press Incorporated
1139 South Wabash Avenue
Chicago, Illinois 60605

This book is printed on 100% recycled paper

The frontispiece and the chapter-opening calligraphy
were done especially for this volume by José Cisneros

ISBN 0-8040-0632-6
LIBRARY OF CONGRESS CATALOG CARD NUMBER 73-1500

To my sister
Peggy

Contents

Illustrations

MAPS

Preface

A general consensus among historians is that biography is the most difficult form of historical writing. At first glance this statement seems far from true. The story is at once firmly circumscribed by the birth and death dates of the subject, and the unfolding of the narrative usually follows a conventional chronological pattern from youthful beginnings, through maturity, to end of career, and a final analysis of character, motives, and contributions. Once the facts of a man's life are assembled, the tale almost tells itself, although, undeniably, the writer's skill is necessary to breathe life into the naked collection of documented pieces and give birth to a cohesive and convincing account.

The first requirement for an author of biography was perhaps best stated by Edward Hallet Carr, when he expressed the belief that "history cannot be written unless the historian can achieve some kind of contact with the mind of those about whom he is writing." It may be self-evident that a biographer must come to know the mind of his subject as closely as possible in order to be qualified to present an accurate and faithful description of his life, but doing precisely that is a task of some magnitude. Of a well-known person of obvious historical significance, much may be known and a good deal already written. In such cases the writer's job is usually one of separating myth from reality, of reexamining the man's career in light of recently discovered information, and of drawing, at last, a more truthful portrait.

In other cases, involving men little known whose contribution to history is not so obvious, the biographer becomes a literary detective, chasing down clues and ferreting out enough details to clothe his framework with sufficient flesh to make a story and convince his reader that the subject is, after all, worthy of attention. Where facts are thin, the author may resort to "telling of the times," and then by an exercise of controlled imagination suggest what his man or woman may have been doing during the period for which no information is available. All this requires a certain expertise in the writer's craft, as well as a fundamental honesty on the author's part, since, as J. Frank Dobie once wrote, "In order to arrive at truth, he cannot, like the novelist, discard those facts that fail to comply with the logic of his character."

The demands upon the biographer, then, are great. If his perspective is balanced and he uses his sources with judicious care and strives for a clean, straightforward prose, he may produce a work of precision that creditably reflects upon his subject. To achieve this it is perhaps useful to keep always before him the inescapable fact that history's judgment of one man's life and career is, in part, in his hands.

MARC SIMMONS
Cerrillos, New Mexico

Introduction

He was called *El Leoncito,* The Little Lion, by the simple *peones* of New Mexico who knew him a century ago. Manuel Antonio Chaves earned that name in more than a score of battles with hostile Navajo, Ute, and Apache, and there can be little doubt that he was one of the finest Indian fighters the Southwest ever produced. Chaves' life straddled three periods of New Mexican history: He was born at the tag end of the Spanish colonial period, he grew to manhood in the rough and heady days of the Santa Fe trade during the quarter century of Mexican rule (1821-1846), and he spent his mature years under the territorial regime established by the United States. Through the workings of fate, or by mere chance, his career was interwoven with practically every major historical event of the epoch in which he lived. Yet, because history is a capricious mistress, Manuel Chaves' name has been virtually forgotten.

In the area of the Spanish Southwest—that vast sweep of country stretching from Texas on the Gulf of Mexico to

California's Pacific shore—now live better than four million persons whose language and culture lead back to Iberia. Spain ruled over this jumble of plains, mountains, and deserts twice as long as the United States has to date, and her influence remains firmly stamped on the land and people.

In spite of some regional interest in the subject, attention given in history books to the work of Spanish pioneers remains meager indeed. Perfunctory treatment is often accorded the explorers and conquistadors who first visited the Southwest, but thereafter, of the men and women who built their homes and held on to them for the next three centuries in the face of incredible odds and hardships, little is said. In part this is attributable to the Spaniard's failure to keep private journals, diaries, or memoirs — the stuff from which the gritty details of daily life can be gleaned. On the other hand, Spanish officialdom had a penchant for proper legal forms and stored up reams of government documents, many of which are still preserved in archives. But what comes across from these impersonal official papers with their bare, white-boned recital of the workings of government has all the blood, sinew, and gristle stripped away. There is much to inform but little to excite the imagination.

The first Anglo-Americans who entered New Mexico and neighboring provinces in late colonial times and during the period of Mexican rule did record much of value concerning people and customs in the personal accounts they composed, but as these men labored under a strong Puritan bias and in some cases an outright prejudice against all things Spanish, their words must be measured with care. For example, in their writings they condemned the moral looseness of Spanish women who had the temerity to appear on the streets of Santa Fe with rouged cheeks and smoking cornhusk cigarettes. They ridiculed adobe houses, which to them looked more like brick kilns than human habitations. Against the Catholic Church they railed because during Mass the priests permitted musicians with guitars and violins to strum and saw away at the same tunes rendered the previous evening at a fandango. They bewailed the corruption of local politics and found offensive the casual manner in which judicial proceedings were handled. And, finally, they wrote disparagingly of the humble New Mexican citizen who appeared to them shabby and cowardly and who seemed to offer sorry resistance to the inroads of hostile Indians.

In their haste to heap scorn, these carping critics with their superficial and sweeping condemnations neglected to report that the Spanish and Mexican tatterdemalions whose bravery they impugned had stood firm for centuries, absorbing the heaviest blows their foes could deliver and defending themselves with no more than antiquated muskets and bows and arrows, all the while bereft of but minimal support from their government and suffering stoically the travail of famine, drought, pestilence, and isolation from the mainstream of civilization. The mere fact that they survived and held the land represented no mean achievement. But this went unrecognized, or at least unacknowledged, when the first Anglo writers set pen to paper. So it is not to them with their lack of sympathy that we should look to find mention of courage and heroism on this far frontier.

From what has been said, it may be understood that the shaping of the story of Manuel Chaves has not been a simple task. A hundred years ago when men still gathered about campfires and storytelling was a well-developed art, his exploits were known to all New Mexicans. Since retelling encourages enlargement and embellishment, the stories became tales, history melted into legend, and Manuel Chaves became something of a folk hero. But only a little of this was ever put down in writing, and when men left their campfires his deeds were largely forgotten.

Manuel Chaves wrote no autobiography, nor did he compose newsy letters to friends, or in any other way record the highlights of his many-faceted career. His eldest son Amado, who was devoted to family history, evidently intended to do a biography but gave up the project when most of his notes and papers were lost in a fire that destroyed the New Mexico territorial capitol in 1891.[1] Ironically, Amado, then Superintendent of Public Instruction, had placed these papers together with some of his father's effects in the building for safekeeping. On several occasions, notably in lengthy letters to historian Ralph E. Twitchell and to Laurence Lee, Amado Chaves wrote from memory concerning his father's life and the family genealogy. Much of this Twitchell incorporated into the biographical sketch of Manuel which appeared in his *History of the Military Occupation of New Mexico*. Amado also knew and furnished information to author Willa Cather when she was in Santa Fe during the early 1920s and working on the novel that would become a small classic, *Death Comes for the Archbishop*. Although Manuel Chaves figures in this work of fiction only as a minor character, the details presented concerning his life are historically accurate.

After Amado Chaves, Charles F. Lummis wrote most extensively and knowledgeably about Manuel. Lummis, who first entered New Mexico in the mid-1880s, was of approximately the third generation of Anglo-American writers. It was he, in fact, who through his books introduced the rest of the nation to the then unknown Southwest, boosting it as an exotic and undiscovered Mecca for tourists and in his enthusiasm coining the expression "See America First." Unlike authors before him, Lummis was generous in his praise of New Mexico's Spanish heritage, and he portrayed the land and people in extravagant terms. A subject that came under his flowery pen more than once was the life of Manuel Chaves. He knew the old campaigner briefly before his death, and in the years following he heard more about him as he traveled throughout New Mexico. Unfortunately Lummis' interest in spinning a good lusty yarn exceeded his dedication to canons of historical accuracy. Late in life he made the bold assertion that "no statements have ever been found inaccurate in my books,"[2] but in truth Lummis was always more of a journalist and popularizer than a historian, and when he waxes eloquent upon the merits and deeds of El Leoncito, the tale emerges with considerable varnish. Nevertheless, his contribution to the present biography is eminently significant.

For the rest, the story of Manuel Chaves has been pieced together bit by bit from period newspaper accounts, from scattered references sifted out of a variety of contemporary writings, from the archives of New Mexico and the National Archives in Washington, and from oral family tradition. Admittedly, the result is not a portrait completely drawn. Gaps remain that probably never can be filled in. And yet sufficient detail has been marshalled to show Chaves' life in some depth and make a convincing case for including him among the ranks of illustrious Southwesterners. Men such as Kit Carson, Billy the Kid, Lucien Maxwell, John Chisum, the Bent brothers, and General E.R.S. Canby have found their biographers, and their names have seeped into the history books, while Manuel Chaves, and others like him, have been neglected and their memory all but lost.

The picture of Manuel Chaves presented here shows a man possessed of spirit and of the ability to think and fight under severe pressure; a man of courage, gallantry, and leadership of a superior order; a man modest and unassuming who was yet quick to hold firm when he felt he was in the right; and a man with capacity for endurance which made him seem impervious to privation and personal suffering. In short, as this book hopes to make clear, El Leoncito was an authentic American hero cut from the pioneer mold, and as such deserves a secure place in our history.

1

Roots

South of Santa Fe and the wedge of high peaks that the Spaniards called the Sangre de Cristo, the Rio Grande slices through a lava plateau and emerges upon the first of a series of flood plains that extend in a string down to El Paso. Where it breaks out of the northern mountains and canyons, the river's rush begins to slacken as the channel widens and irrigation canals siphon off their needs and reduce the volume of the mainstream. As the valley begins, so does the Bosque Grande, the Big Grove, a venerable forest of cottonwoods that shade the river banks for 150 miles. For centuries Pueblo Indians and Spanish farmers camped in the Bosque, gathered wood for their fires, and at selected spots tilled the fertile alluvial soil which lies beyond the fringe of the trees. When the first frost of autumn sweeps down off the mountain tops, the leaves of these old cottonwoods are touched with gold and become stiff and papery, so that any gentle wind can set them to dancing and chattering.

As the Rio Grande toils its way southward, the signs of man become more common. Farms and villages and towns appear, the houses low and flat-roofed, stuccoed with the rich brown soil dropped by the river on an earlier journey. Fields, long and narrow strips of green ribbon, lead back from the *acequias* or irrigation ditches as far as the sandy, desolate edge of the valley. Horses and cattle and a few belled goats wander through the Bosque cropping the thin shoots of grama grass or drift out onto the desert flat to sample the salt bush and leafy mesquite.

Opposite the craggy bulk of Sandia Mountain on the east, the Rio passes Albuquerque and a dozen lesser communities before continuing on to disappear in the dust laden haze of the south. Albuquerque today is a metropolis edging toward a population of 300,000. Few of its citizens now are dependent on the river for irrigation; most in the daily round of their lives are scarcely conscious of its presence. Insulated and isolated as we are from the simple and primitive, it is difficult to recall that on this same stretch of river bank a century or two centuries ago dwelled other people whose life style and whose view of their world and themselves was entirely different from our own. They watched the crest of the river and saw the hovering peak of Sandia as we may still do, but their thoughts were turned to problems of Indian raids, smallpox epidemic, famine, or flood. We cannot relive such times—would not want to—but we can learn something about those who did, admire their courage, sympathize with their failings, and marvel at the tenacity which allowed them to achieve some success here upon the margin of civilization on this rawest of frontiers.

Spanish colonists began ranching in the area around modern Albuquerque as early as the mid-seventeenth century. But they left for El Paso at the time of the disastrous Pueblo Indian revolt of 1680, so that the formal founding of the community known officially as the Villa de San Francisco Xavier de Albuquerque was not made until 1706. This occurred during the reign of Don Francisco de la Cueva, Duke of Albuquerque, who was viceroy of New Spain, of which New Mexico formed the northernmost province. The new *villa* or town, in assuming the viceroy's name, sought to honor this highest and most illustrious of New World officials, and perhaps at the same time to acquire a measure of recognition by linking itself to a noble title.

Yet hopes for greatness or prosperity which the founders of Albuquerque may have entertained were never realized, at least in colonial times. To the end of Spanish rule the community remained an unspectacular place with little to distinguish it from towns of like size elsewhere in the province. There was a plaza of sorts, as one would expect to find in any settlement of Spaniards, and, of course, a church. The first church, established soon after the villa's founding, stood on the west side of the plaza, and records show that an individual named Don Antonio de Chávez[1] was obliged to contribute several hundred adobe bricks to its construction in order to receive a dispensation to marry his cousin. This initial building was neglected by the Albuquerque parishioners and it collapsed in the 1790s. A new one was raised shortly afterward at the present location on the plaza's north side.

Near the plaza and the church were grouped the houses of a few of the municipality's residents. As late as the 1770s, these dwellings numbered only twenty-four, for most families had strung their homes northward up the river valley to be near their fields. Southward through the Bosque lay the inhospitable swamps of Mexia, shunned by the colonists for agricultural purposes and used only for occasional grazing.

On the west bank of the Rio Grande, directly opposite Albuquerque and two musket shots from the river's edge, was the small community of Atrisco. Then a satellite of Albuquerque, today it is a suburb. The name Atrisco is a corruption of the Aztec word *atlixco* meaning "upon the water" and as a place name has its origin in the Valley of Atlixco in central Mexico. A few hardy souls were probably already tilling the soil at Atrisco when Albuquerque was laid out in 1706. In any case, it was the latter which came to dominate this section of the valley and Atrisco, mostly because of its position on the west side of the river, remained relatively isolated and somnolent.

The priest of Albuquerque's San Felipe church was required to minister to the spiritual needs of the Atriscans, but owing to the lack of a bridge and the dangers attendant upon swimming or boating the river, he was usually unable to fulfill his obligations. The good father who was serving in 1760, for example, declared that he was under constant apprehension and that when the river froze it was necessary to cross on the ice and "when the ice thundered he thought he was on the way to the bottom, because when he crossed, it creaked as if it were about to break."[2] So although the plazas of Albuquerque and Atrisco were no more than a league and river apart, communication between them was infrequent and uncertain.

On the west where Atrisco's plots of corn, wheat, squashes, beans, *punche* (native tobacco), and chile reached their limit, cholla-studded sand hills rose in gentle undulations toward the irregular line of the low lava shelf or mesa that marked the perimeter of the Rio Grande Valley on that side. Five small volcanos, their dark cones lined in an orderly row, soldier fashion, stood sentinel on the mesa summit watching and perhaps brooding over the generations of human activity in the valley below.

The view the villagers had to the west was impeded by this mesa and the volcanos, but if they climbed the heights they could easily look over into the Rio Puerco Basin with its monolithic rock formations and see the compact mass of the San Mateo Peaks beyond. They probably did this frequently to scout the country, for this was the direction from which their enemies most often came—Navajo, Ute, or Gila Apache, bent upon theft of flock or herd or the seizing of captives.

Of the details of everyday life in colonial Atrisco, there remain but few. What little is known suggests that the pattern of existence here was indistinguishable from that in dozens of other New Mexican hamlets distributed along the river. This otherwise nondescript community arrests our attention, however, because here on October 18, 1818 there was born to Julián Chaves and to his wife María Luz García a son, christened Manuel Antonio.[3]

The Chaves clan was an old and distinguished one in New Mexico, and long before its service here had registered significant achievements in mother Spain. The family name can be traced to the twelfth century when the Spaniards were in the midst of their long crusade to expel the infidel Moors from the Iberian peninsula. In the year 1160 Christian attention focused on the small town of Chaves located on the Rio Tamega in extreme northern Portugal and ten kilometers below the Spanish border.[4] The King of Spain, Don Alonzo Enríquez, had attacked Chaves on repeated occasions in an effort to wrench it from Moorish hands, but without success. The bravery of the defenders and the

City of Chaves, now in Portugal. *Photo from Amado Chaves collection.*

Portion of original wall of Chaves, Portugal, stormed by the López brothers in the year 1160. *Author photo.*

Chaves family escutcheon. *Photo courtesy Fray Angélico Chávez.*

stout walls, through which passed five gates, seemed to render Chaves impregnable.

Two young hot-bloods, cousins of the King, decided to try their skill and luck. They were Ruiz López and Garcí López, who raised an army in Portugal at their own expense and besieged the town. After a series of bloody battles, the prize was taken in a furious assault which resulted in death by sword for most of the enemy. Upon learning of the victory, the King hastened to Chaves accompanied by his queen and two daughters. The surviving Moors were exiled, and in an elaborate ceremony the monarch bestowed a series of honors upon the pair of triumphant brothers. They were knighted, made members of the Military Order of Santiago, presented fine Andalusian horses and saddles, and golden spurs were placed on their feet by the royal princesses. The King, in an expansive gesture, gave them the town of Chaves and ordered that, henceforward, the designation "de Chaves" should be added to their name and that their heraldic crest should bear five keys on a field of crimson. "Chaves" means keys in Portuguese; the number five represented the gates which had been stormed; the red field indicated the town had been taken in battle. In this manner Chaves became the name of one of the leading warrior clans of Spain.[5]

To commemorate the famous victory and honor the López brothers, an inscription in gold letters was placed in an arch of the town's principal church, setting forth the details of this notable event. Several centuries later the exploits of the López de Chaves brothers received further recognition from one of their own descendants, Don Luís Zapata de Chaves (1526-1594), who recounted their achievements in an epic historical poem, *Don Carlos Famoso*.[6]

From the twelfth century onward, those who bore the

Chaves name distinguished themselves in Spanish history, and with the opening of the New World their valorous deeds were carried to another theater. A Juan de Chaves was one of the leading captains of the conquistador Pedro de Alvarado in the exploration and colonization of Central America. In the later sixteenth century, Don Gabriel de Chaves served as *alcalde mayor* or chief political officer of the province of Veztitlán in southern Mexico. And the adventurer Nulfo de Chaves became the first European to penetrate the rugged Chiquitos and Matto Grosso districts of South America.[7]

Of more interest to our story is Don Pedro Gómez Durán y Chaves who in the year 1600 appeared as a sergeant among the troops of Juan de Oñate, founder of the Spanish province of New Mexico. This individual, progenitor of the Chaves family on the northern frontier and a lineal descendant of the old crusader Ruí López, was a native of the village of Llerena in Spain's desert province of Estremadura. At the time of his appearance in the upper Rio Grande Valley, he was described as "a well-built man of good features, fifty years old, and the legitimate son of Hernán Sánchez Rico."[8] A decade later Don Pedro was down at the port of Acapulco on Mexico's west coast where he was entrusted with taxing the cargo of a ship bound for the Philippines. Shortly thereafter he must have returned to New Mexico, for by his own testimony he was one of the founders in 1610 of the Villa of Santa Fe, the provincial capital.

Through his own enterprise, and perhaps because of his noble family name, Don Pedro Durán y Chaves soared to prominence, becoming a major landholder in the area north of Atrisco and by 1626 the *Maestre de Campo* or Field Marshall of all the king's troops in New Mexico. A curious fact, denoting his prestige in the community, was that he and his descendants appended the title of "Don" to their names, a privilege which otherwise was accorded only to the governor during the seventeenth century. At a later time the title was conceded to all landowners and magistrates, and finally in the nineteenth century to almost any man reaching advanced age.[9]

Don Pedro sired two sons and a daughter. The eldest of these and heir to the family title and property was Fernando Durán y Chaves who became lieutenant-governor of New Mexico and political administrator of the Rio Abajo, or the jurisdiction's southern district. One of his sons, Fernando Durán y Chaves II, was a military officer at the time of the catastrophic Indian revolt in 1680, and with other survivors of the now extensive Chaves clan he fled with his wife and children south to El Paso. Of all the Chaves males, only Don Fernando II returned with his family to the upper Rio Grande Valley with General Diego de Vargas at the time of the reconquest in 1693. This event may well have marked the high point of his career for De Vargas presented him with the coveted office of *alférez real* or high sheriff and royal standard-bearer for the grand *entrada* into the newly rewon city of Santa Fe. Of this event General De Vargas entered in the official record,

> I, the said Governor and Captain-General, about the eleventh hour of said day [December 16, 1693], made my entry into this Villa of Santa Fe . . . with the squadron on the march and in the company of the very illustrious Council of this the said Villa and Kingdom, its high sheriff and color-bearing alderman, the Captain Fernando Durán de Chaves, carrying the standard referred to in these acts, and under which the land was conquered. . . .[10]

Thus did this Chaves carry on the proud military tradition established by his forebears in medieval Spain.

During the thirteen-year exile of the New Mexican settlers at El Paso, almost all members of the House of Chaves moved southward to the more peaceful provinces of northern Mexico, where their progeny may be found to this day. It was left, therefore, to Don Fernando Durán y Chaves alone to re-establish the family stock in New Mexico. In so doing he founded the parent stem of numerous generations which succeeded him in this arid and remote land.

A great, great grandson of the high sheriff and royal standard-bearer was Don Julián Chaves, who probably would have gone unremembered had he not become the father of one of the Southwest's finest Indian fighters. Although the exact year has been lost, Julián must have been born toward the end of the eighteenth century, and if not in Atrisco, then most likely in one of the several farming villages below Albuquerque where the Chaves name predominated. Of his life history little is known, except that he was one of several children and the son of Don Pedro de Chaves and Doña Catalina Baca, who were natives of the town of Tomé.[11]

Concerning a sister of Doña Catalina, María by name, who would have been the maternal great-aunt of Manuel Chaves, there remains a curious and tragic story. The tale still forms part of the oral tradition of the Tomé district, and although some details show that history and legend merged, the main outline is amply documented by Church and Spanish archival records.

In the third quarter of the eighteenth century, the Comanche, Navajo, and Gila Apache were wreaking havoc upon the Rio Grande settlements: plundering fields, seizing herds of livestock, and on occasion pillaging small hamlets, slaying the men and carrying off women and children. Of these offenders none was more dreaded by the pioneer family than the Comanche, whose reputation for ferocity was unmatched by any other tribe. But the Spaniard's fear was mixed with a certain grudging respect, for the Comanche were widely acknowledged to be the bravest and noblest Indian with which they had to contend. This may help to explain why the settlers accepted a truce from these Indians at certain periods each year for the purpose of peaceful trade. At such times representatives of both parties mingled freely in the bartering of goods, the Comanche passing unmolested in and out of the Spanish towns, with their hosts doing likewise in the tipi villages set up nearby.

Weeks or months after termination of the truce, the Comanche might return to the same towns where they had been hospitably received and carry out the most bloody and damaging raids. And doubtless their work was made easier by information they had gleaned from an inside view of Spanish defenses. Notwithstanding, the settlers looked with favor upon the truce period since it offered a welcome, albeit brief, respite from attack and provided opportunities at which efforts could be made to try and convince the Comanche to accept a year-around peace.

Such were the conditions when a large Comanche village arrived on the outskirts of Tomé one year in the mid-1770s. The leading spokesman for the Tomé citizens at this time was Don Ignacio Baca, upon whose shoulders fell the duty of overseeing trading activities as well as opening talks which might lead to a permanent cessation of hostilities. On this occasion prospects suddenly loomed brighter than at any previous time. The Navajo, implacable enemies of the Comanche, had been especially troublesome in recent months, and Don Ignacio began pressing for an agreement with the Comanche chief to join hands against the common foe. He must have applied all his persuasive powers for the Indian was won over and Tomé achieved the friendship of the Comanche which it had sought for so long.

The chief was accompanied by his son, a sturdy lad of ten, who spent the afternoons playing with Don Ignacio's seven-year-old daughter María. To cement the new alliance the Indian suggested to his host that they pledge their children in marriage so that both peoples would become one and together fight their common enemies. Ignacio Baca saw the value of such an arrangement, and the pact was sealed. In succeeding summers the Comanche returned to Tomé to renew their friendship and present gifts of horses, buffalo robes, and jerky to María and her family.

When the Comanche youth became nineteen, the entire band descended on the town bearing even more splendid gifts and prepared to celebrate the long-awaited wedding. But there was a rude surprise. Don Ignacio had changed his mind. Indian hostilities had been abating in recent years and the friendship of the Comanche and the old alliance with them no longer seemed of great importance. Besides, the Don belatedly was moved with doubt concerning the wisdom of throwing his daughter's life into the hands of pagans.

As a result Don Ignacio sent his child to visit relatives in the village of Valencia and when the Comanche arrived in festive attire, he met them with a mournful face. Leading the chief and his son to the cemetery, he pointed out a fresh grave, claiming that the girl lay there, a victim of smallpox. The Indians were familiar with this disease since they too had frequently suffered from its ravages, so the story seemed entirely plausible. And lamenting the loss of María they departed in great distress for their own country to the east.

Sometime later a party of traders from the Indian pueblo

of Isleta, which was situated not far north of Tomé, undertook a journey to the plains to barter with the Comanches. When the Indians spoke of the death of María, the Isletans expressed astonishment. Not so, they said. She was alive and well for they had seen her within the week.

Not long afterward the people of Tomé were assembled in the parish church to celebrate the feast of Santo Tomás, their village patron. A rush of horses' hooves outside was the first warning of danger, followed by a loud disturbance at the door. Suddenly the church was filled with painted Comanches who fell with their old savagery upon the defenseless people. The priest dropped upon the altar riddled with arrows, while the other men, Don Ignacio among them, were felled where they stood. The women were rounded up and carried away into captivity and Tomé was left a smoking ruin. Another priest was hastily summoned from Albuquerque to bury the dead and offer comfort to the few wretched survivors. Tomé had paid many times over for the duplicity of its leading citizen.

María, the innocent cause of so much bloodshed, spent the remainder of her life as the wife of the Comanche to whom she had been promised. Several other Tomé women were taken to Texas by the Indians and eventually, after ransom or escape, appeared in New Orleans.[12]

It is curious to note that a grandson of María known as Puercus was a chief of the Comanche in the middle 1860s when he visited Puerto de Luna on the Pecos River with a small band of warriors and two of his wives. It is recorded that there he met Colonel Manuel Chaves who was at the peak of his career as one of the most celebrated fighters in New Mexico. Were the two men aware that they were cousins? Probably, since the story of the Tomé massacre was still a familiar one a hundred years after the event. As Puercus' band left Puerto de Luna on its way to rejoin the main camp, it was set upon by a Navajo war party, and after a determined resistance every one of the Comanches was killed.[13]

The wife of Julián Chaves and mother of Manuel was María Luz García de Noriega, herself descended from early Spanish colonists. The first of her ancestors in New Mexico was Alonso García, a native of Zacatecas, who arrived during the mid-seventeenth century. His son, a noted soldier during the Reconquest, was later killed by the Apaches.[14] Through the years members of the family were in the front ranks of those who served in defense of the province. Among their number was Captain Francisco García de Noriega, the father of María Luz.[15]

The old baptismal records are incomplete for the Atrisco parish, so the exact number of children Julián and María Luz had is unknown. Besides Manuel, the most famous of their offspring, the couple brought forth at least three other sons. José, probably the eldest, early met a tragic death at the hands of the Navajo in an incident which also very nearly claimed the life of Manuel. Of another son, Pedro, the only detail known is that he married Asención Chaves in 1831 at the Village of Cebolleta.[16] Finally, a younger brother of Manuel, named Juan, is mentioned in family records and he too apparently met an untimely end.

As a child Manuel Chaves must have played among the giant cottonwoods bordering the Rio Grande and listened around the night fires of winter to the legion of tales that composed the Chaves family history. He probably did his share of chores, for responsibility settled early on the shoulders of New Mexican youth. His father Julián was a successful stockman and farmer who, according to a later family tradition, brought home the first alfalfa seed tied up in a cotton blanket, part of his purchase on a trip to Chihuahua. The alfalfa was planted in the vegetable plot near the house and the tender shoots and leaves were eaten as greens.[17]

We can be sure that Julián Chaves considered himself fortunate to have stalwart sons coming along who could help care for the family properties. He, like all New Mexicans, hoped for a large household as the only defense against the constant toll taken by war and disease. In later life Manuel claimed he could tick off the names of two hundred relatives, near and distant, who had been slain by Indians. Since he was kin to practically everyone in the province, this statement certainly was no exaggeration, and better than any other it conveys some notion of the magnitude of the cloud under which these plucky New Mexicans constantly lived.

2

Youth

When Manuel was nine years of age, Julián Chaves took his wife and children to live at the village of Cebolleta, forty miles west of Atrisco at the foot of the San Mateo Peaks. The reason for this move is not known. It may have been a simple need for more pasture land to accommodate increasing flocks of sheep. Or perhaps some misfortune or difficulty in Atrisco drove Julián to seek a fresh start among relatives who resided at Cebolleta. The possibility remains, of course, that he was lured on by the love of adventure and danger inborn among so many of the Chaves men. In any case, the move was to prove an important one in the life of young Manuel, for a hazardous boyhood spent in a frontier town was to be the crucible which produced in time a skilled and resourceful fighter.

When Julián Chaves and his family took up their new home in the late 1820s, Cebolleta possessed a short but blood-stained history. Early in the year 1800, thirty families from the crowded area south of Albuquerque had come westward to the small, well-watered pocket of a valley long known to the Spaniards as Cebolleta or "Little Onion." The name derived from the wild flowers of the onion family which flourished along a small stream.[1] West of the valley the view of lofty San Mateo Mountain and its surrounding peaks was shut off by the angular wall of a pale yellow mesa, but eastward toward the Rio Puerco Basin the country fell away in a vast sweep of distance broken only by two conspicuous landmarks. One was a dark volcanic plug called Cerro Negro and the other a lava-encrusted butte known as Cerro de la Celosa or Jealous Woman Peak, named for a legendary Navajo who jumped from its heights after losing her husband to a rival.

The first settlers of Cebolleta, as they selected a town site and marked off the limits for a plaza, were acutely aware of what they might have to endure before this land could be irrevocably won. Although they held a formal grant issued on January 31, 1800, by the Spanish governor in Santa Fe, none could forget that the Navajos had long claimed this region and thus far had successfully excluded all intruders. In anticipation of attack, the town fathers ordered the construction of a fortified plaza with houses built contiguously around the central square: doors and windows facing inward with only loopholes opening on the outside, and a single passageway, protected by heavy pine gates, giving access to the interior. In similar fashion were most of the frontier villages in New Mexico built during the later colonial period.

When the adobe and rock fortress was complete, imposing as it was, some of the Cebolletans remained apprehensive about its capacity to withstand serious assault. Their position forty miles from Atrisco and Albuquerque and on the extreme western rim of Spanish settlement was almost too

Street in the village of Cebolleta today. Ruins of the original defensive wall on the left. Here Manuel Chaves spent his boyhood. *Author photo.*

Ruins in the village of Cebolleta today. In the background is the yellow mesa or escarpment that extends west to the San Mateo Peaks. *Author photo.*

A sheep camp in the mesa country near Cebolleta. During the nineteenth century shepherds spent months at a time in such isolated camps, exposed to attack by Navajo and Apache. *Author photo.*

Laguna Pueblo. The Indians of this village were neighbors of the Cebolletans on the south and gave them refuge after the Navajo attack in 1804. *Courtesy Museum of New Mexico.*

remote to receive battle aid in a pinch. A dozen miles to the south was the Pueblo of Laguna. Although the Indians here were friendly to the whites, they had their own problems with the Navajos and could scarcely be counted upon to back up the settlers if hostilities ensued. It was apparent then that Cebolleta's walls and the courage of its citizens stood as the principal bulwarks protecting the town.

From the beginning as the people plowed new fields along the diminutive stream, herded their flocks of sheep and goats, and gathered firewood on the cedar- and piñon-freckled mesas, they suffered harassment from the Navajos and occasionally from wandering war parties of Utes and Jicarilla Apaches drifting down from the north. Robberies and murders were commonplace, and the cemetery grew faster than the town. Still the incidents were isolated, and the victims were those caught away from Cebolleta's protective walls. But what all feared most was a concerted Navajo drive against the community itself. A formal request was made to the governor in Santa Fe for a detachment of troops, but all that could be spared from the undermanned garrison in the capital were several soldiers commanded by a corporal. Even so, the arrival of these men was a welcome addition to Cebolleta's defenses, since they brought a small number of muskets which were distributed to the citizens.

By 1804 the Cebolletans, having weathered four years of small raids, were gaining confidence in their ability to hold the town. In fact they may have been growing complacent. But on September 16 of that year the long-delayed blow fell. A thousand Navajo warriors appeared in the valley and the settlers hastened into their fortress, driving their livestock into the plaza and barring the gate.

For days the town was besieged, the Indians raining

arrows upon the rooftops and hurling flaming pitch-pine knots over the walls. From this desperate battle were born tales of individual heroism destined to become part of the historical legacy of succeeding generations. In one instance, a middle-aged woman, Doña Antonia Romero, narrowly averted disaster. Like other women she had been making bandages, carrying water to the men, helping soothe the terrified livestock, and beating out fires and dispersing smoke. During one attack she crept up on a flat roof to view the fighting from behind a parapet wall. Suddenly she was horrified to see that a Navajo had managed to slip inside undetected and was removing the bar of the gate. With no time to summon aid, she snatched up a heavy *metate*, the stone basin for grinding corn, which had been put out of the way on the roof. Heedless of the arrows sailing about her, Señora Romero ran to the edge and threw down her burden, crushing the warrior's skull. The gate and town were preserved.

A more grisly story concerned Don Domingo Baca, one of the toughest of the Cebolleta fighters. He was with a party of volunteers that sallied outside the walls and engaged the Indians in hand-to-hand combat. In the thick of battle a Navajo rushed at him with a lance and ripped open his belly. Baca staggered back into the town, grabbed up a pillow, lashed it over the gaping wound, and returned to the fray where he was seen firing his musket until the fight subsided several hours later. When he removed the pillow, his friends standing about were aghast, and quickly made the sign of the cross as for one already dead. But Baca returned the dangling entrails to their proper place, called for needle and sinew, and sewed up the wound himself. These crude ministrations proved effective, for he recovered and lived to fight again.

The Navajos finally abandoned the siege, so the Spanish records tell us, after losing twenty-two killed and suffering forty-four wounded. But, although the Cebolletans had won a victory of sorts, they had little cause to rejoice. Their own casualties included the loss of their corporal and the wounding of most of the remaining soldiers plus a dozen townspeople. In fact the strain of the prolonged engagement and the certain knowledge that the Indians would soon renew hostilities so depressed the settlers that after some debate they decided to give up the town.

According to the terms of their original grant, however, they were prohibited from leaving without permission of the government. While such license was being sought, the Cebolletans packed up their meager goods in *carretas*, two-wheeled carts, or on burros and moved south to Laguna Pueblo for security. The Spanish governor in Santa Fe received the petition of the colonists and was greatly moved by the description of their sufferings. Nevertheless, it was strictly against royal policy to abandon frontier zones once they had been claimed, and without making a final decision he referred the matter to his superior, the military commandant in Chihuahua. The commandant also felt sympathetic toward the Cebolletans, but in an official order he decreed that the law must be obeyed and that they should return to their homes. To allay their fears, however, he agreed to send a troop of thirty soldiers from Chihuahua to protect them.

Upon receipt of this order the settlers left Laguna and returned to their walled town. Shortly they were heartened by the arrival of Lieutenant Nicolás Farfán and his men from Chihuahua who had been dispatched in fulfillment of the commandant's promise. In the following year, 1805, the Navajos again descended upon Cebolleta, but were easily driven off with the aid of the soldiers. Although the citizens were plagued by Indian troubles for another fifty years, they thought no more of retreat.[2]

These remarks on the early history of Cebolleta are necessary to show the character of the community in which Manuel Chaves was to pass his youth. They also demonstrate that whatever the reason which led his father to uproot the family from its home in Atrisco and move to the perilous country below San Mateo Mountain, it must have been a compelling one.

Nature was far from prodigal in its gifts to the Cebolletans, and young and old alike toiled unremittingly to bring corn, beans, goat meat or mutton, cheese, and chile to the table. The boy Manuel surely contributed his full share to support of the Chaves family in its new abode, tending sheep, turning soil in the fields, and packing burros high with wood collected on the mesa top. When the daily round of labor allowed time for diversion, Manuel, his brothers, and the other youths of Cebolleta found sport in developing their proficiency with weapons and their skill in horsemanship. There was no powder and ball to be frittered away on target practice with the town's Spanish flintlock muskets, but resourceful boys could make their own bows and arrows, and knives and steel-tipped lances could be had when the men went to the Rio Grande settlements to trade. Endless hours were consumed in contests: piercing chips of wood with arrows, driving a knife blade into a circle on a tree trunk from forty feet, racing bareback on horses pell-mell over the roughest terrain, and making up wrestling matches and foot races. The grim seriousness with which the boys went about their war games was in keeping with the very real danger from Indians who felt their homeland was being unjustly invaded and settled. And the youthful contestants themselves were aware that strength and skill gained one day in play might save their lives on the next in war.

Specific information on Manuel's first years in Cebolleta is fragmentary. It is known that his older brother Pedro took a wife from the branch of the Chaves clan that had originally settled the town, for the marriage records of the Catholic Church show that on April 13, 1831, he wed Asención Chávez.[3] This same brother twenty years later was slain by Indians in San Miguel Canyon several leagues west of Cebolleta.

Sometime shortly after the wedding festivities, the father, Julián Chaves, died. Whether his demise resulted from natural causes or from a brush with Navajos is not certain. By early 1833 at the latest his widow María de la Luz married a prominent Cebolletan, Don José Antonio Baca. Doubtless, Manuel's new stepfather was a close relative of the doughty warrior Domingo Baca who, a quarter century before, had sewed up his own stomach. This marriage was soon rewarded with a son, and Manuel had a half brother, Román Antonio Baca, whose future career was to be bound up closely with his own.[4]

One aspect of Cebolleta's history that has not been touched upon and that was linked to an important event in the life of Manuel Chaves concerns the proclivity of that town's citizenry to engage in slave raids against the Navajos. How early the practice began and to what degree it inflamed the Indians against the townspeople is difficult to ascertain. Slaving expeditions were common in New Mexico during colonial times and fully accepted as just retaliation for Indian raids. Since this activity was strictly forbidden by Spanish law, the colonists carefully avoided designating their captives as slaves and referred to them euphemistically as *criados* or servants. In fairness it should be noted that hostile Navajo, Ute, Comanche, and Apache in a like manner seized Spanish captives for their own use, and numerous instances existed of these becoming completely acculturated and reconciled to Indian life.

The sketchy records available strongly suggest that slaving was practiced by the Cebolletans from their days of first settlement in the Navajo country. In any case, by the mid-nineteenth century it was firmly fixed as a way of life, so that most New Mexican communities recognized a band or company of men known as "Cebolleteños" whose principal occupation was stealing Navajo children to sell in other towns. By established custom, whenever a wealthy father arranged for the marriage of a daughter, he commissioned the "Cebolleteños" to bring in a Navajo boy or girl to be given as a bridal gift. Moreover, youths of Cebolleta and other border villages often went on forays alone or with a few loyal companions to secure a captive child to serve their own bride-to-be. Since such enterprises were attended with considerable risk, many young swains failed to return. Manuel's son Amado, writing about this business in later years, mentioned laconically,

> On arriving home [after a slaving expedition] the first thing to do was to take the children to the priest to baptize them and give them a name. They would naturally take your name and as they grew up they would consider you and your wife as their parents. If you did not have the pluck to go after Indian children yourself you could buy one for five hundred dollars. It must be remembered that many parties that went after servants never returned. The Indians killed them all.[6]

In the mid-1830s, apparently when Manuel was about sixteen, his elder brother José assumed leadership of fifteen Cebolletan youths who formed an expedition to visit the

Navajo county. One source says that the young men's motives were entirely peaceful as indicated by several mule loads of trade goods which they assembled.[7] Since the New Mexicans often went successfully into the country of hostile Indians to trade, this is perhaps not implausible, although a relationship which permitted friendly intercourse between avowed enemies appears strange today. In this particular case it is more realistic to put faith in other accounts which assert that the purpose of the expedition was slave-taking.[8] It may be that at the beginning the young adventurers' aims were flexible: if they found the Navajo strong and vigilant their mule-borne merchandise might gain them safe passage through the country. On the other hand, if the Indians were scattered in isolated camps, they might find opportunities for snatching up captives and carrying them with other booty and their own trade goods to the Rio Grande towns for disposal. In any event, when the trader-slavers filed out of Cebolleta with José Chaves in the lead, the boy Manuel marched with them, quite likely in the capacity of warrior apprentice, since this was his first ride into the heart of the enemy's domain.

West of Cebolleta a well-worn trail climbed upward and then wound across the broad tableland which jutted northward from the base of the San Mateo Peaks. On the far edge of this escarpment members of the party paused before taking a steep path leading down and surveyed the sweep of desert that melted into violet haze and the blue ridge of the Chuska Range. Not many miles to their right they could see a soaring volcanic plug Alesna, the Awl, whose sharp pinnacle served as a guidepost to travelers headed in or out of the Navajo country. Descending a rocky trail, the Cebolletan youths passed below the mouth of San

Alesna, the Awl. This volcanic plug on the plains northwest of the San Mateo Peaks served as a landmark for early New Mexicans visiting the Navajo country. *Author photo.*

Miguel Canyon and emerged on the salt bush and chamisa flats under the shadow of Alesna. From this point on, every league they traveled put them deeper in the enemy lair and beyond the pale of help from home.

The number of days José led his companions westward has not been recorded, but it must have been something under a week. In all this time they saw no sign of Indians and the singular matter was discussed around the evening fire. Where were the Navajo? Had they moved their flocks of sheep to better grazing? Or had they perhaps gone into hiding to escape the Apache? Questions were put to Pahe, an Indian boy raised in Cebolleta and brought along as camp tender. But he had no answers and merely shrugged.

With growing apprehension and perhaps a foreboding of doom, the young men continued to steer a westerly course. When they reached the brink of an awesome chasm, probably Canyon de Chelly in eastern Arizona, the puzzle was solved.[9] The Navajo had gathered by the hundreds on the floor of the abyss to feast and conduct a religious ceremonial. Dozens of campfires sent up plumes of white smoke, a great chorus of voices rose over the muted rhythm of drums, and far down the canyon, where rock walls receded and a valley widened, could be seen an impressive herd of Indian horses. José Chaves must have recognized the peril instantly and he ordered retreat. But Navajo scouts had already detected the *Nakais,* as they called these enemies, and by signaling they brought warriors swarming up over the canyon rim.

The battle was short and bloody. The youths for all their rashness were able and manly fighters and they resisted like cornered panthers. Early in the affray the boy Pahe received a chest wound and unseen crawled away among the rocks. José Chaves fell under an avalanche of arrows.

Manuel must have fought with the best of them for when he finally dropped to the ground unconscious he had sustained seven wounds. As the last of the shooting sputtered out, the Navajo, who themselves had suffered eighteen casualties, went over the field and took what pleased them in weapons and goods. Believing all the *Nakais* were dead, they abandoned the corpses to the buzzards and returned to their feasting and dancing.

With the fall of darkness the cool night air revived Manuel and he staggered about the battleground searching for his brother. He discovered Pahe, whose injury did not appear to be serious, and together they located the body of José, dragged it to a sandy arroyo, and using their hands scooped out a shallow grave. The only course now open to them was a staggering one—afoot and without arms or provisions, the two boys, both weakened by the loss of blood, would have to try and reach Cebolleta almost two hundred miles to the east. Whatever legacy in hardihood had been granted to Manuel Chaves by breeding and environment now asserted itself and he started homeward, Pahe trailing behind.

The pair traveled all that night, rested the following day, and with diminishing strength took up the road again in the evening. Manuel was swinging in an arc somewhat to the south in hopes of hitting a well-known watering spot, Ojo del Oso or Bear Springs. Thus far they had not seen any Navajos; they seemed to have remained bunched up at their ceremonial camp, but there was always the chance that the boys might fall prey to stray hunters or a war party returning from the New Mexican settlements.

On the morning of the second day they reached Bear Springs, a cold clear pool tucked away in a cove off a larger valley which skirted the northern edge of the Zuñi

Site of Bear Springs looking toward the Wingate Valley. The oak trees that sheltered young Manuel Chaves after his escape from the Navajo about 1834 have died and the spring-fed pool that refreshed his body has disappeared. *Author photo.*

Mountains. Luxuriant grass carpeted the margin of the spring and a stand of trees offered shade. The boys had eaten nothing since the day of the battle, and their hunger drove them to pull spines from pads of prickly pear and chew the fibrous cactus. Manuel stripped off his blood-encrusted clothes and lay in the icy waters. At first his wounds opened and bled freely, but soon they closed and he crawled out on the grassy bank much refreshed. Pahe's wound had begun to fester, but he refused to enter the water and instead peeled the soft buckskin film called *carnaza* from the inside of his moccasins and used it to patch the hole in his chest.[10] Manuel fell into an exhausted sleep and awoke many hours later only to discover his companion had died. Dragging the dark and bloated body away from the spring, he covered it with brush, the best burial his feeble strength could afford.

Alone now, the lad summoned his full measure of resolve and set himself toward the east. What transpired during the ensuing days and nights remained in his memory afterward only as misty, dreamlike fragments: endless placing of one foot before the other . . . a pain-wracked body . . . drops of his blood spattering on rocks . . . a coyote or a phantom dogging his trail . . . moccasin tracks leading to a tiny pool of fetid water . . . gnawing of more cactus pads . . . visions of home and his mother.

Manuel wandered delirious into the bowl of a wide valley northwest of San Mateo Mountain and collapsed in the shelter of an oak grove. When he regained consciousness some of the fever had left him, though his wounds were still puffy and hot. He must have lain there awhile mustering his slender reserves, and perhaps, if the conviction had not abided with him all along, he decided he was going to make it. We know some moment of significance passed as he lay stretched under those leafy boughs, for decades later when the Navajo were subdued, he would return to this very oak grove, build a ranch and, on the spot where he had rested, erect a chapel.

Two days later, as Manuel worked his way across the same tableland that he and his companions had traveled on their way out, he fell in with shepherds from his own town. They bore him home on a litter and Cebolleta learned how the flower of its youth had perished.

One other incident, possibly apocryphal in part, remains to be told with regard to this episode. During the absence of the ill-fated expedition, two blacksmiths, Ramon Sena of Santa Fe and José Castillo of Cebolleta, had gone north for the purpose of taking silver jewelry to a friendly camp of Navajos who were separated from their western tribesmen. By some communication the Indians there learned of the battle at Canyon de Chelly, and fearing for the safety of the two smiths, the headman of the camp sent them back to Cebolleta escorted by some of his young men.

The townsfolk meantime had heard details of the tragedy from Manuel and assumed that the two blacksmiths had also been massacred—thus their astonishment when Sena and Castillo rode into the plaza with their entourage. The Navajos were fed and offered shelter for the night, but several Cebolletans led by Manuel's brother Pedro plotted to kill them in their sleep in retaliation for the youths who had lost their lives. When Manuel heard what was planned, he left his sickbed, had his mother assemble weapons, then awoke and armed the Navajos. Confronting his brother, in sharp language he advised him to give up his intention and leave their guests at peace. By dawn cooler heads among the Cebolletans took charge and an escort of volunteers was formed to conduct the Navajos half way back to their own camp. Although Manuel's role in this small drama appears melodramatic and tests one's credulity given his recent ordeal, it is in keeping with the character he displayed on later occasions.[11]

3

Fugitive

In the small isolated villages of New Mexico a century ago it was not uncommon for persons to spend their entire lives within a few miles of the place of their birth and to die without having visited a populous town such as Albuquerque or Santa Fe. To be sure, merchants aplenty traveled yearly down the Camino Real to the markets of Chihuahua and Durango, and New Mexican buffalo hunters often went to the plains for hides, tallow, and meat. Also militiamen ranged many miles from home when called upon by the governor to join campaigns against troublesome Indians. But for the most part the simple rural folk remained wedded to their fields and flocks and knew of life in the provincial capital and other towns only through hearsay of travelers.

It would have not been surprising, then, had Manuel Chaves as he approached manhood remained at the family hearth and dedicated himself to farming or stockraising. Except for occasional slaving escapades, this was the path followed by most youths of Cebolleta. But Manuel did not stay at home, for he had received a full measure of adventuresome blood from his forebears. His mettle had been severely tested on the hard anvil of the ill-conceived Navajo expedition, and perhaps the fact that he alone survived that tragedy furnished evidence that his rigorous training combined with strength of character had produced a man destined to play some greater role in the world beyond the limits of his boyhood village.

In late 1836 or early 1837 Manuel went to Atrisco to visit his grandmother. Probably he had come back to this, his birthplace, on other occasions since his family's move to Cebolleta, but this trip was significant since it represented a break with home. After a stay in Atrisco, he seems to have journeyed downriver, partaking of the hospitality of other members of the Chaves clan and meeting relatives he had not seen before. According to one story, which cannot be confirmed, he encountered a party of German merchants along the Rio Grande who were en route from Sonora to New Orleans with a packtrain of wares. The traders engaged the boy as an *arriero* or muleteer and in this capacity he traveled to the great metropolis at the mouth of the Mississippi, returning within a few months to Atrisco.[1]

At this point, mid-1837, New Mexico was in the throes of a political convulsion which threatened the entire province with civil war. Since independence in 1821, a small clique of wealthy and socially prominent families had controlled the principal government posts, including the governor's office in Santa Fe and those of the several district officials and magistrates. This had been possible because New Mexico, whose status was that of a territory within the Mexican republic, was remote from Mexico City, and the central authorities had been content to let the frontier folk fend for themselves. Therefore, until 1835 New Mexico's governors had been native sons of influential name who received confirmation of their appointment and occasional instructions from the national capital, but who in effect managed affairs very much to their own liking. All this changed early in that year when Colonel Albino Pérez of the Mexican army was unexpectedly named governor of New Mexico and commander of its military forces. Pérez, of haughty mien and brassy manner, arrived in Santa Fe on May 22 to take up his new duties. Looking with disdain upon the bumptious and provincial-minded New Mexicans, he gracelessly snubbed the leading pillars of the community who already held him in suspicion because he was an *extranjero*.

The new governor's position was further weakened the following year when a conservative faction gained control of the national congress and imposed a centralist constitution, abolishing the traditional liberties of the states and territories and concentrating power in Mexico City. It thus fell to Pérez to implement the new regimen of government as it applied to New Mexico.

The immediate issue which embroiled the governor in controversy was one of taxes. Under the old system virtually no direct taxes had been levied upon the people, but now the government made clear that imposts would be placed on various goods and businesses to provide federal revenue. The common folk were alarmed by rumors which magnified the severity of the impending tax, and by one story given wide credence which averred that a man would soon be taxed each time he climbed into bed and coupled with his wife.

Opposition to the governor and resentment against the

new measures boiled over not in Santa Fe, where the citizenry had adopted an attitude of passive hostility, but among the villages of the Santa Cruz Valley some twenty miles north of the capital. Here in early August of 1837 a group of insurrectionists, composed mainly of poor farmers and Pueblo Indians, issued a *pronunciamento* attacking the centralist plan and its tax program and creating a "canton" government to rule New Mexico. In response to this revolutionary movement, Governor Pérez mustered a small force of reluctant followers and confidently marched north to disperse the rebels. Near San Idlefonso his little army was routed and he was forced into flight toward Santa Fe. The following day, seized by an enraged horde of his enemies, he was decapitated and his head was thrown upon a field where it was used in a game of football. Other members of the governor's staff were slain in an equally barbarous manner and their heads, impaled on lances, were paraded about the Santa Fe plaza as trophies of the revolution.

With the death of Pérez, leaders of the movement selected a buffalo hunter of Indian ancestry, José González, to serve as governor of New Mexico. From what little is known of González, he appears as a simple and well-intentioned man who opposed further violence and who sought to negotiate with the central government for a restoration of order and the abolition of taxes. Unfortunately, González, who was both illiterate and politically naive, failed to reckon with counter-revolutionary forces within the territory which began almost immediately to align against him.

As much as the old aristocratic families of Santa Fe and Albuquerque had disliked Albino Pérez, they were in no mood to support a rabble movement which defied established authority and usurped the governor's chair. At first they feared the unruly revolutionists would sack the capital, but actually, once mob fury had been spent on the hapless leaders of government, a decorous order prevailed. The Rio Abajo, the downriver district below Santa Fe, had scarcely been touched by the turbulent events in the north, but there, where some of New Mexico's wealthiest citizens maintained their haciendas, plans were soon underway for the formation of a counter-revolutionary army. A leader in this work was Mariano Chávez, an uncle of Manuel Chaves, but the man who assumed direction of the military forces and who would play the largest role in deposing "Governor" José González was Manuel Armijo. When troops were assembled for the beginning of a drive against Santa Fe, numbered within the ranks was young Manuel Chaves, who, embarking upon his first formal enterprise as a soldier, was as enthusiastic as any volunteer.[2]

Some word must be said regarding the extraordinary Manuel Armijo, since for the next decade his weight would bear heavily in shaping the destinies of both New Mexico and Manuel Chaves. Born about 1792 of a humble family near Albuquerque, he spent his youth tending sheep.[3] According to tradition, he amassed considerable wealth through theft of livestock and by the early 1820s was a man of some importance. By all accounts his rise to prominence was founded on cunning and duplicity rather than personal merit, his ambition leading him at opportune moments to gain a political role in the management of New Mexico's affairs. In 1827 he was appointed governor of the territory but served at that post only until 1829, when he apparently resigned to avoid a federal investigation of irregularities in the conduct of his office.[4] Following this setback in his career, he devoted attention to development of a hacienda near Albuquerque, all the while keeping close watch on matters in the capital.

Governor Manuel Armijo. *Courtesy Museum of New Mexico.*

When the revolt against Albino Pérez burst forth in 1837, Manuel Armijo's name initially is mentioned among the conspirators. He must have hastened to Santa Fe, for by some intrigue he ingratiated himself with the revolutionary leaders, doubtless with the hope of regaining the governorship. But as soon as the selection of José González became known, he quit the movement and returned to Albuquerque in a huff. There, upon assessing the strength of those opposed to the new regime, he adroitly about-faced and made known his readiness to put down the recent disturbances which threatened the "civic peace, harmony, and good order" of New Mexico. On September 8, a group of well-known citizens assembled at the town of Tomé just below Albuquerque and issued a *pronunciamento* calling for vigorous suppression of those forces dedicated to anarchy. Armijo was the first to affix his signature and rubric to this document. Therein he had been named leader of the troops with his cousin Mariano Chávez designated as second in command.[5]

As far as reputation and personal integrity went, Mariano Chávez stood poles apart from Armijo. He was born in 1808, the son of Francisco Xavier Chávez, who in 1822 became the first governor of New Mexico upon establishment of the Mexican Republic, succeeding the last Spanish governor, Don Facundo Melgares.[6] Mariano was related to Armijo through the latter's mother, who was a Chávez, and through two brothers who married into the Armijo clan at Ranchos de Albuquerque. When Mariano Chávez himself wed Dolores Perea of Bernalillo, he became linked to another of the most powerful families in the territory —the Pereas, owning immense flocks of sheep and maintaining hundreds of *peones* on their baronial estate.[7]

Mariano's Hacienda de Padillas was the largest along the river south of Albuquerque. His lands embraced extensive cottonwood groves and pasture land on both sides of the Rio Grande and his sprawling adobe ranch house flanked by huts of his Mexican workers and Indian servants was protected by stout mud walls with loopholes. Nearby was the hacienda of his merchant brother Antonio José Chávez, who was to be slain by outlaws on the Santa Fe Trail in 1843. Susan Shelby Magoffin, visiting Mariano's home in 1846, the year after his death, described its elegant furnishings and showed that, at least for the *ricos* or aristocrats, life on the raw New Mexican frontier was far from cheerless:

> The house is very large . . . with handsome Brussels carpet, crimson worsted curtains, with gilded rings and cornice, white marble slab pier tables—hair and crimson worsted chairs, chandelabras. And all the Mexicans have the greatest passion for framed pictures and looking glasses. In this room of Chávez's house are eight or ten gilt-framed mirrors all around the wall. Around the patio are chambers, storeroom, kitchen and others. All is exceedingly neat and clean.[8]

At the assembly of citizens held in the village of Tomé on September 8, 1837, Mariano Chávez, as a person of rank and influence, addressed the gathering and called for prompt action against the Santa Fe rebels and their governor José González. In his remarks he declared, "I know of no one better qualified to lead our army than General Manuel Armijo; therefore I ask this assemblage to declare him to be our leader."[9] And without a dissenting vote this was done.

As Armijo mustered his army, he virtually stripped the Rio Abajo of firearms and of men able to do military duty. Consequently many of his officers and men, fearing for the safety of their families and possessions if left unprotected, packed up their households and conveyed them by cart or muleback in the wake of the advancing troops. Mariano Chávez must have been included in this number—at least we find a short time later that his young son José Francisco, who would grow up to be a renowned Indian fighter and statesman, was attending a small school in Santa Fe. Probably Manuel Chaves assisted his uncle's family during the march to the capital, although likely he had official duties as well.[10]

By September 12, Manuel Armijo occupied Santa Fe, which the rebels had vacated upon his approach. José González fled to Taos with a few partisans, while the men who had constituted his army returned to their homes to begin the fall harvest. Armijo at once sent couriers to Mexico with an exaggerated account of his personal exploits and within a brief period won confirmation as the governor of New Mexico and commander of its military forces. Dismay in the national capital over the upheaval in New Mexico prompted the authorities to dispatch two hundred dragoons to assist Armijo, who now appeared as the savior of the territory, in quelling any further disturbance and in bringing the leaders of the insurrection to account. With the arrival of these soldiers, Governor Armijo in January 1838 marched north to attack the rebels who had again collected in large numbers in the Santa Cruz Valley. With their backbone stiffened by the presence of the Mexican dragoons, his troops engaged the enemy at Pojoaque Pass and emerged victorious. José González, captured near Santa Cruz, was allowed a few moments to make a hasty confession to a priest and then, under orders of Armijo, was stood up before a firing squad. Four other leaders of the revolt were shortly afterward executed in Santa Fe.[11]

Exactly what part Manuel Chaves played in these events has not been recorded, although we may assume he was a participant in or observer of the principal episodes which witnessed Armijo's return to power. Over the next two years he seems to have divided his time between the capital and the Hacienda de Padillas. In all likelihood the latter served as his main residence after leaving Cebolleta. In a document of April 23, 1839, listing new commissions for the rural mounted militia, Manuel Chaves is named as a sub-lieutenant (*alférez*) in the Company of Padillas.[12] It may be, too, that during the years when he was based at his uncle Mariano's house, Manuel received some kind of informal schooling. Later events in his life demonstrate that he was literate, and certainly no academic training had been available during his boyhood in Cebolleta.

At least by 1839, if not before, Manuel Chaves was being drawn into an association with Governor Armijo which would soon involve him in a series of remarkable incidents. From all indications the governor was amicably inclined toward his youthful kinsman, and perhaps recognizing him as a man of promise tried to draw him into his circle of supporters.[13]

However, a strange episode which probably took place during the fall or early winter of 1839 brought a temporary halt to harmonious relations between the two Manuels. Chaves at this time undertook an extended visit to Santa Fe, accompanied by his young half brother Román Baca. The pair were welcomed and feted in the homes of several of the best families and, doubtless, many hours were spent in company with the governor. Manuel Chaves, who already enjoyed some small fame owing to his near-miraculous escape from the Navajos, was even better known for his fine horse Malcreado, a racer bred out of solid old Spanish stock. The New Mexicans of this period were exceedingly earnest in their dedication to horseracing, and nothing gained universal approval in quicker time than possession of a mount that consistently could win bets for its owner. American traders and merchants entering New Mexico invariably expressed amazement over the excitement generated by any gambling event, whether open-air card games on the Santa Fe plaza, cockfights, or races.

Manuel's Malcreado, which had been run on Saint's Days and at fiestas in villages all along the Rio Grande, owned a well-deserved reputation, and his appearance on any field was sure to draw a crowd. Governor Armijo also possessed a fleet horse of which he was quite proud, and one day, engaging in friendly argument over the respective merits of their animals, the two agreed to a race. The day was set several weeks hence to give both men a chance to bring their horses to peak condition, and a substantial amount of money was wagered. Chaves either had funds won in earlier contests or borrowed from friends to match the governor's bet.[14]

It appears certain that Manuel Chaves had enough reservations concerning the character and motives of his kin that he set brother Román to keep constant watch over Malcreado. Each night the horse was locked in a stall together with the boy who spread his blankets on a pile of straw. Yet as events proved, even these precautions were unavailing.

Among citizens of the capital, Manuel Armijo had gained a name for shrewdness and hard dealing, while his moral imperfections were common gossip. His pomposity was exemplified by a favorite saying attributed to him: *Dios en el cielo y Armijo en la tierra* ("God rules the heavens and Armijo rules the earth"). Although he had an upstanding wife in Trinidad Gabaldón, whom he had married in 1819, he frequently was seen consorting about town with Doña Tules Barceló, a notorious demimonde who operated a gambling hall. Doña Tules, one of Santa Fe's more intriguing personalities during the tumultuous decade of the 1840s, was born in the Mexican province of Sonora. Sometime before 1820 her family emigrated to New Mexico, and Tules (diminutive form for Gertrudis) grew up in the village of Valencia south of Albuquerque. In the summer of 1823 at nearby Tomé she married Manuel Antonio Sisneros, who, coincidentally, was a brother of the maternal grandmother of Manuel Chaves.[15] The couple moved to Santa Fe where Sisneros shortly afterward left his wife and went to the village of Manzano to live. Doña Tules, thrown upon her own resources, capitalized on her handsome appearance and fondness for cards. The gambling den which she opened became a popular resort for members of the social elite, and as mistress of Governor Armijo she was held in certain awe by lesser members of the community. The success of her establishment was due in no small part to her expertise in dealing monte, and within a few years she acquired a substantial fortune.[16] The irascible Armijo she handled with velvet gloves and managed to stay in his favor until his political demise in 1846.

When the horserace with Manuel Chaves became known, many persons expressed readiness to place bets on the outcome. Armijo, perhaps with a knowing wink, assured Doña Tules that any money she might wish to lay on his entry would be perfectly safe. But more he would not say. In fact, he had already settled upon a plan to achieve by skullduggery what he felt sure he could not win by honest competition.

The key figure in Armijo's conspiratorial design was Dr.

Philippe Auguste Masure, popularly known about Santa Fe as "the French doctor," but in reality a Belgian by birth. He had emigrated with his brother Henry to St. Louis in 1827, where he established himself in practice by offering through a local newspaper "his professional services in different branches of physic, surgery, and midwifery."[17] In 1831 the brothers moved to the Mexican frontier, Philippe settling in Santa Fe, while Henry, also a physician, continued on to Sonora. In the New Mexican capital, Dr. Masure found a ready need for his talents. Securing quarters with John Scolly, a former Kentuckian who operated a store on the plaza, he administered to the needs of the American merchant colony as well as the great and humble among native residents.[18]

There exists, fortunately, some record of what transpired in a secret meeting that Governor Armijo arranged with the French-speaking doctor. We may assume that the august and corpulent presence of His Excellency completely intimidated Masure, who is known to have been slight, almost delicate in physical carriage, and diffidently polite, with sandy hair and whiskers. What Armijo proposed in forceful terms was that the physician employ his skill upon Manuel Chaves' Malcreado in such a way as to insure that it would not cross the finish line before the governor's horse. In plain terms, the race was to be fixed. Although he was promised $1,000 for this bit of deviltry, Dr. Masure was probably moved to accept the commission more out of fear than greed.[19] In any event, he bowed to the governor's will.

According to what he later related to Manuel Chaves, the doctor went to the stable in the small hours of the morning before the race. Through a window he observed the horse and the guard, Román, asleep on his pallet. Soaking a rag with some kind of anesthetic, he tied it to a pole, passed it through the window and held it over the boy's nose until he was unconscious. Then crawling in through the window, he administered the horse a slow acting poison.

The day dawned crystalline clear and Santa Fe was thronged with expectant racing fans. Word had spread to the outlying settlements, and people hastened to the capital for a chance to bet and to observe what might well prove the leading sporting event of the year. The race course lay to the south of town on a level, treeless piece of ground where Indians from the plains usually pitched their tipis when visiting Santa Fe. A track a thousand yards in length had been designated and a rope stretched across the finish line. As was customary in such contests, it was understood that once the horses started, unexpected mishaps would be given no consideration in determining the winner.

Besides the personal wager between Armijo and Chaves, betting was heavy among the spectators. In the excitement of the moment, women wagered their jewels and some men their entire fortunes. Most of the money favored Malcreado, since young Manuel assured friend and stranger alike that his horse could not be beaten. Armijo in a jovial mood covered all bets.

Manuel Chaves, although an expert rider himself, had decided that Román should be his jockey, leaving him free to stand with the judges and governor and keep a close surveillance over the proceedings. Román, light and agile and giving no hint of the three-hundred-pound bulk of a man he would become, dispensed with saddle and climbed aboard Malcreado bareback.

On signal the two animals leaped forward and a great shout burst from the crowd. The Chaves horse swiftly took the lead and, with Román glued to his back riding low, moved far ahead with long easy strides. It appeared to onlookers that this was not a race but a runaway. Then fifty yards from victory, Malcreado faltered and suddenly fell. Román managed to leap clear as Armijo's steed thundered past and dashed across the line.

The spectators were stunned. The race was over and lost to the governor, yet for the longest moment there was not the slightest sound from the huge throng. Ashen-faced Manuel Chaves slowly walked out on the track as Román got to his feet beating dust from his clothes. It was apparent to all that the horse was dead. Suddenly on every side people began muttering that they had been misled and betrayed and Manuel heard threats against him. Shamed and bewildered, he could do nothing but escape the field as quickly as possible. Governor Armijo, appearing strangely unconcerned over the tragedy that had befallen his rival, went among the crowd with a few friends, gathering a rich harvest.

The affair, however, was far from closed. Chaves, at a loss to explain why fate had dealt with him so harshly, brooded over his misfortune for several days. Then he had an unexpected caller, and as he listened, his perplexity changed to wrath. Dr. Philippe Masure sat before Manuel Chaves and admitted the poisoning of Malcreado. The man was distraught, fear-ridden, and perhaps remorseful. Besides explaining how the governor had pressured him into the crime, he added that after the race Armijo had given him only $300 of the amount promised and repudiated the balance. When he complained, the governor had reviled him as "a damned rascal and a bad citizen" and ordered him to leave the country or he would have him shot. Was it genuine regret on the doctor's part or a desire for revenge against Armijo or perhaps hope for protection that led him to seek out Manuel Chaves and make his woeful confession. Whatever his motive, it bore no interest for Manuel. Once he had the story, it was directly to Governor Armijo that he went to seek an explanation and redress.

Confronted with Manuelito's accusation, Armijo merely laughed. He held the government, the town, the entire territory in the palm of his hand and he was not about to demean himself by returning lost bets and making a public apology. Further, he threatened stern reprisals against a certain French doctor, and he had no objection if Manuel wished to carry a warning. A less determined youth might have ground his teeth in frustration, smothered his pride, and left the arrogant governor secure and smug to enjoy the fruits of his contrived victory. Not Manuel Chaves.

The young man went straight for his weapons, selecting a bow and quiver of arrows he often used in matches with friendly Indians. When night blanketed the town, dropping pools of black shadow in the lee of adobe walls, he stepped from his house and headed for the central plaza. Suspecting that Armijo might be keeping a rendezvous with Doña Tules, he hid in the murky darkness alongside the Governor's Palace, hoping for a chance to waylay him. But the governor made no appearance that night and Chaves returned to his quarters in the early morning hours before dawn, fully intending to stalk his prey again that same evening.[20]

Somehow, though, Armijo found him out. One account says that Doña Tules learned of the planned assassination and carried word to her paramour; another that one of Chaves' friends, becoming drunk, betrayed him. In any event, Armijo raged and bellowed about the Palace like an old bull. No young upstart, relative or not, was going to trifle with him, and he declared himself ready to pay $5,000 to the man who delivered Manuelito's head to his office. What a stir that somber announcement created as it swiftly circulated about the capital. One of the first to hear was the would-be assassin, who entertained little doubt that Tio Manuel would have his head if he could. The governor was as vindictive as he was powerful, and though Manuel was no coward, he promptly decided that discretion dictated flight. He may briefly have considered returning to Cebolleta or his uncle Mariano's hacienda at Las Padillas, but knowing the length of Armijo's arm, likely no place in the territory could afford him real security. So taking another of his fleet-footed horses, alas it could not be the lamented Malcreado, he rode east out of town, bound for the Missouri settlements and exile in the United States.

Hungering for revenge, Armijo set a troop of soldiers on the trail as soon as news of the flight reached him, but Chaves, bred to the ways of the Indian, easily eluded them. Somewhere out in eastern New Mexico he struck the Santa Fe Trail and fell in with an American caravan heading home after the summer's trade. By agreeing to tend the animals and perform camp chores, he gained safe company across the plains, two meals a day, and a berth at night under a wagon: good fortune for a penniless fugitive who was going to have to depend upon his wits in a strange country. It is not unlikely that Dr. Masure was also a member of this same train, since it is known that he too fled the territory and shortly turned up in Missouri.[21]

Upon reaching the hamlet of Westport Landing on the banks of the Missouri River, Manuel's duty with the caravan ended. Here were a scattering of rude log cabins, several clapboard houses, and a handful of stores, blacksmith and wheelwright shops, and grog parlors, offering little in the way of interest or opportunity for a lad in need of winter employment. Polite inquiry soon revealed that further east in St. Louis he might find a suitable position, and without hesitation Manuel sought the road thither.

Situated strategically near the junction of two mighty steams, the Missouri and the Mississippi, St. Louis was the nerve center of the middle border and the great commercial entrepôt for the Indian and Mexican trade, as well as the principal market for the mountain men who harvested the fur of the Far West. We may be certain that the rustic country boy from New Mexico was properly awestruck as he beheld the hurly-burly of this bustling metropolis and mingled in its streets with the colorful array of frontiersmen, merchants, river boatmen, teamsters, shop keepers, soldiers, and visiting Indians. In its strangeness St. Louis offered much to delight the eye, but for Manuel during his first days in its midst there must have been pangs of homesickness, adrift and friendless as he was in a foreign city. Withal he was not one to abandon himself to despondency, and before long he learned of a wealthy Spanish merchant, Navarro by name, who was knowledgeable in the ways of this place and who might be willing to steer an enterprising youth into gainful employment.

Señor Navarro, indeed, proved accommodating. He personally had need of many cords of firewood, as did others, and if Manuel could find and organize workers to supply this fuel he would be assured of a comfortable profit. He further volunteered the information that outside the city were camps of Mexicans waiting in idleness for spring to join caravans bound for Santa Fe and Chihuahua. Here was a work force ready made.

Elated, Manuel made his way to the Mexican camps where, with little delay, he enlisted a company of woodchoppers. Next he made arrangements with the old mercantile family of Chouteau to cut timber from its properties, and with this, Navarro offered him a formal contract to deliver sixteen hundred cords of wood. Prospects were suddenly looming brighter for a winter in exile.

It is evident that from the onset Señor Navarro took a great liking to his young protégé. Quite probably he was acquainted with, or at least knew by reputation, some of the Chavezes who were involved in the Santa Fe trade and who made periodic trips to St. Louis. If Manuel was of the same character and industry as his relatives, any efforts to aid him would not be wasted.

By spring Manuel had proved his worth. The contract fulfilled, he paid off the crew, and was left with several hundred dollars, a not inconsequential sum for that time. Moreover, he was beginning to master English, the lack of which had been a serious handicap. In some manner he met a handsome and intelligent young Cuban, Alfonso Fernández, who persuaded him to form a partnership for the operation of a fruit store. So into the venture went Manuel's hard-earned lump of capital. Just what the Cuban contributed, if anything, is unclear.

By mutual agreement Fernández assumed the role of proprietor over the new store while Manuel became the buyer, spending much of his time plying the Mississippi to and from New Orleans where he purchased great quantities of fruit. The business was attended with such success that the two young novices were well on their way to becoming rich. In an expansive mood, Manuel wrote to his younger brother Juan in New Mexico inviting him to join a summer caravan and come to St. Louis. Some months later the boy arrived and was placed in school at Manuel's expense.

The prosperity of the new business, however, was destined to be short lived. Alfonso Fernández apparently was endowed with more charm than honesty, a fact which Manuel might have gathered from his friend's fondness for card games. One source attests that the Cuban had extraordinary luck at his games and used the winnings to expand the firm's assets. If so, it may have been a change in that luck which first suggested an altogether different approach to the fruit business.

One day Manuel returned from New Orleans to find the store closed and his partner gone. Investigation revealed that Fernández had liquidated the company stock, emptied the till, and fled to New York. If Manuel Chaves was the kind to seek revenge upon the governor of New Mexico, he was certainly not the sort of man to dismiss lightly this new betrayal, and after selling the boatload of fruit brought from New Orleans he set out for New York. On reaching that city, he discovered the faithless Fernández, one leap ahead of him, had already taken ship for Cuba. Very well, he would go to Cuba too, although his money was dwindling alarmingly. But once on the island, Fernández' home ground, he lost the trail completely. After suffering the ravages of a tropical fever, Manuel made his way back to St. Louis, chagrined and a good deal wiser regarding the untrustworthiness of his fellow men.[22]

In Missouri Manuel took stock of his position. Once again as upon his initial arrival, he found himself fundless, but now he knew his way around, possessed friends, and had a fair command of English. Brother Juan could no longer be sustained in school, but the ever obliging Navarro found a place for him in his store. This arrangement was most agreeable to the boy, for school work was tedious, and while clerking proved scarcely more adventurous, it did offer a chance to see his employer's daughter, with whom he had become smitten.

At what labor Manuel maintained himself during the ensuing months is not known. By the spring of 1841 he had been absent from his native land for almost a year and a half, and the desire to return was strong in him. But for all he knew, Armijo's offer for his head still stood, so thoughts of home, he felt, must be put aside. About this time, however, a caravan of New Mexicans arrived in Missouri, the first of the season from Santa Fe, and with it came word that boded a significant change to the good in Manuel's situation.

Commerce between Missouri and New Mexico over the Santa Fe Trail had begun in 1821, when William Becknell, "father of the trade," led the first packtrain of mules across the plains to the Rio Grande. The Mexican settlers, starved for manufactured goods that their mother country could not supply and willing to pay in silver, furs, and mules, offered a ready market for enterprising Yankee merchants. For the first five years, the Missouri traders with their huge caravans of Murphy and Conestoga wagons dominated the transcontinental business. By 1826, however, some of New Mexico's more capable citizens decided to intrude upon this monopoly, and organizing their own freight trains, they embarked for the eastern settlements to procure goods and bring them back to Santa Fe and other provincial towns. These native entrepreneurs, prominent among whom were the Armijos, Chávezes, and Senas, succeeded in avoiding the usual custom duties that bore so heavily upon their Yankee competitors, but even so, their operations were limited, capturing only part of the market, and the bulk of the profits still went to the men from Missouri.

The train that reached St. Louis early in 1841 was owned by Ambrosio Armijo, a relative of the governor, and Antonio José Chávez, who was accompanied by his brother Mariano.

When Manuel heard of the arrival of his uncles, he was overjoyed, knowing that soon he would have news of Santa Fe, of the hacienda at Las Padillas, and perhaps of Cebolleta. The two Chávez brothers were heavily involved in trade between the United States and Mexico, meshing this mercantilism with their ranching activities along the Rio Grande. Antonio José, before he was robbed and murdered in present Lyons County, Kansas, in 1843, usually handled the Missouri end of their commerce, while Mariano superintended the export of goods from New Mexico south to Chihuahua. It is recorded, for instance, that Mariano sent $26,474 worth of merchandise to Chihuahua in 1844, and later that season exported 6,000 sheep worth $3,000 to the same place.[23] Mariano may have accompanied his brother to St. Louis on this trip to assist in making purchases or perhaps just to see the sights. But either explanation could have served merely as an excuse, since his real purpose was to confer with his favorite nephew, Manuel.

Something is known of what passed between the two and it appears as a truly extraordinary exchange. After the usual pleasantries and swapping of news, Uncle Mariano broached the subject that had led to this meeting. Governor Armijo had undergone a change of heart. He was willing to forget the past, cancel the reward offered for Manuelito's head, and allow the boy to return home. Mariano handed his nephew a letter which contained a pardon and a guarantee of safety. Manuel ran his eye over the paper and snorted. He believed he knew the governor too well to trust his word. Within twenty-four hours of his appearance in Santa Fe, he could expect to be shot, guarantees notwithstanding.

Apparently Mariano had expected some reaction such as this. "Listen," he said, "I know you cannot trust Armijo, but you can trust me. I promise you that he will not harm you, and you know whether my promise amounts to anything or not."[24]

Still skeptical, Manuel pondered these words carefully. He was well aware that Manuel Armijo respected, perhaps feared, only one man in all New Mexico—Mariano Chávez. His uncle, he knew, often berated the governor for the capricious manner in which he handled his office, and Armijo's only response when another moralizing lecture began was to declare, *Dejen a Mariano está enojado* ("Better let Mariano have his way if he gets angry.")[25]

Manuel, nevertheless, remained suspicious of Armijo's motives. Why this sudden turnabout? Mariano Chávez himself was not sure of the answer, but he had a guess. Rumblings were being heard along the border between New Mexico and the Republic of Texas. The Mexican authorities, as yet unreconciled to the loss of their Texas province in 1836, sent repeated messages to New Mexico's governor, warning of impending trouble, and Armijo was in a constant state of apprehension. Perhaps, Mariano suggested, Governor Armijo, looking ahead, saw a possible need for the services of a bright young man, already battle proven and conversant in English. It was as plausible an explanation as any.

In the end Manuel was won over. He had become thoroughly sick of St. Louis, and although his exile had had its pleasant moments, he was eager to view again the brown sage-studded expanses and rock-ribbed mountains of New Mexico. He bid goodby to Juan, who by now, completely enamored of Navarro's daughter, had decided his future lay in this city. As the brothers parted, Manuel to accompany his uncles back to New Mexico, they little realized they would not meet again. Manuel Chaves never returned to Missouri, and Juan, after marrying his inamorata and fathering two girls, was drowned in a boating mishap on the Mississippi. As the caravan of New Mexicans threaded its way westward, Manuel stretched his muscles in the labor of trail and camp and reflected that the young man who had come this way nearly two years ago as a fugitive was going home as a full man.

4

Santa Fe

In 1838 Mirabeau B. Lamar was chosen president of the Republic of Texas. The vote was almost unanimous, since the two other candidates committed suicide before election day. Lamar succeeded the popular hero Sam Houston who had led Texan forces to decisive victory over Mexico at San Jacinto in 1836 and who had been prevented by the new constitution from seeking the presidency for a second two-year term.

President Lamar at once expressed the aim of his administration: "to promote the true basis of all national strength and glory."[1] In a message to the Texas Congress he called upon the people to "elevate our young Republic into that proud rank which her unrivaled beauty and unbounded wealth entitle her to take among the nations of the earth."[2] These effusive words were spoken in sincere and patriotic fervor by a man dedicated to carving out an empire from an untamed but potentially rich wilderness. The strong nationalism which Lamar espoused was intended to promote a greater Texas, but it also conveniently served to distract attention of citizens from such real problems as Indian raids, threats of invasion by Mexico, and a bankrupt treasury. Until the government managed to overcome weaknesses inherent in infancy, it could offer little but pride in nationhood and promises of a bountiful and secure future.

Lamar, through his plans for empire, envisioned a Republic of Texas stretching from the Gulf of Mexico to the Pacific. Actually, in the days of Mexican rule, Texas' eastern border had been basically what it is today, and her western boundary had been open and ill-defined, merging at some unknown point with the province of New Mexico. A shadowy basis perhaps existed for a Texas claim to eastern New Mexico by virtue of a declaration made by the First Congress of the Republic in 1836 which preemptorily fixed the national boundary as the Rio Grande from its mouth to its source. This took in the city of Santa Fe and much else that no stretching of legal points could ever concede to the ownership of Texas.

Nevertheless, early in 1840, Mirabeau Lamar boldly embarked upon the first stage of his grand design to extend his borders westward. On April 14 of that year, he addressed to the people of Santa Fe a letter brimming with cordiality and calling attention to the prosperity which, he claimed, Texas had enjoyed since casting off Mexico's tyrannical yoke. With unbounded generosity he invited the New Mexicans to accept "full participation in all our blessings. The great river of the north [Rio Grande], which you inhabit, is the natural and convenient boundary of our territory, and we shall take great pleasure in hailing you as fellow citizens, members of our young Republic, and co-aspirants with us for all the glory of establishing a new happy and free nation."[3] That these words were written with something less than full sincerity may be gathered from Lamar's known aversion to Mexicans whom he considered "an inferior people, not to be trusted."[4] In any case, Manuel Armijo, chief recipient of this message in Santa Fe, was not deceived.

More than a year elapsed before President Lamar was in a position to proceed further. But by June 19, 1841, he caused to assemble a force of 321 men at a camp north of Austin. To this day the precise mission of the little army, known to history as the Texan-Santa Fe Expedition, remains hazy. Apologists affirm that its ends were peaceful—to extend the jurisdiction of Texas over New Mexico only if the citizenry was willing and to explore possibilities for opening trade between the two regions—and deny that it was an expedition of conquest. Certainly the ostensible purpose of the soldiers, under the command of General Hugh McLeod, was to escort the several Texan commissioners who bore papers from President Lamar to the Santa Fe authorities and to protect from the Indians a small group of sightseers accompanying the expedition. Yet, no matter the real intentions or motives of the men from Texas, Manuel Armijo chose to interpret their presence on his soil as an armed invasion and a hostile act by an enemy nation.

When the governor of New Mexico learned of the approach of the Texans, he took measures to arouse his people and place his military forces, both regular and militia, in full battle readiness. He had anticipated such a threat for some time and had long since alerted the government of neighboring Chihuahua to be prepared to lend aid. Scouts were posted along the eastern frontier to spy on the Texan advance, and tight restrictions were placed on the travel of Americans living in the province to forestall any possible communication with the enemy. Finally, Armijo began formulating plans for taking the field in person. In a crisis such as this, he felt, a true leader could inspire his subjects and his soldiers by riding at the head of the army, bedazzling all eyes with plumed hat, tunic, and golden epaulets. Nor did he see any incongruity in the fact that he intended to be mounted on his best saddle mule. As preparations proceeded, Armijo named the men who would compose his staff during the coming campaign. Among those receiving an appointment was his nephew Manuel Chaves, now once again very much in the governor's good graces.

In just what manner Manuel made his reconciliation with Armijo upon arriving from St. Louis is not known. Likely the young man returned quietly to his old haunts, and the governor, marshalling his resources to combat the imminent invasion from Texas, sought out an opportune moment to summon him to the adobe palace. When he assessed Manuelito's wary but unhostile mood, he offered him the post of secretary and interpreter of the field army, whose organization was almost complete. And Manuel, probably with a show of enthusiasm, accepted.

By early September of 1841 Captain Damasio Salazar, commanding a military patrol on the Pecos River, sent word to Santa Fe of the capture of several Texan scouts and the approach of a large body of the enemy. The prisoners were shortly dispatched to Armijo, and in an interview, quite likely with Manuel translating, the governor learned that the Texan-Santa Fe Expedition had fallen on hard times. Wandering uncertainly but in a general westerly direction across the Staked Plains of West Texas, the invaders had suffered blistering heat, starvation, thirst, attacks by savage Kiowas, and collapse or loss of much of their livestock. Upon approaching eastern New Mexico, General McLeod had halted his column and sent an advance party forward with Commissioner William Cook to meet the New Mexican authorities, profess the peaceful intent of the expedition, and attempt to secure supplies for his distressed men. When Armijo learned these details, he must have smiled with satisfaction realizing the grueling march had done much to soften up his foes. Apparently he brushed aside any suggestion that these Texans had come in peace.

Deciding the moment had arrived for New Mexico's Napoleon to take the trail, Governor Armijo, astride his mule and arrayed in a brilliant blue uniform, mustered his troops and marched grandly out of Santa Fe. Along the roadside some thirty miles east of the capital, he encountered a party of his men bringing in five other prisoners. Among them was Captain William P. Lewis, a young artillery officer, who, fearing for his life, claimed he was a merchant from the United States. At that unlikely declaration, Armijo grasped Lewis by the collar of his dragoon jacket, dragged him up alongside his mule, and pointing to a button on which were a star and the word "Texas," he thundered, "I can read 'Texas' and no merchant from the United States travels in a Texan military jacket."[5] Placing the prisoners under guard in his train, the governor then continued another forty miles to the village of Las Vegas, where he established temporary headquarters.

In the meantime Commissioner Cook and the advance party of Texans, from which Captain Lewis and his companions had separated, reached the Gallinas River south of Las Vegas and near that stream's junction with the Pecos at Anton Chico. There they blundered head-on into several hundred Mexican troops under Captain Salazar who immediately called for their surrender. Since their scouts had not returned, the Texans were unsure of the attitude of officials in Santa Fe and of the treatment they might receive if they laid down their arms. While they studied their position and Salazar's demand, a body of reinforcements arrived on the opposite side of the river and joined the Mexican command. This proved to be troops from Armijo's main army that had hastened down in advance of the governor to provide support for Salazar's men. Their appearance much dispirited members of the expedition whose enfeebled condition and recent sufferings had scarcely left them in condition to engage in serious battle.

As the camps faced each other, two men detached themselves from the Mexican line and drew toward the Texan officers and Commissioner Cook. At a distance, the latter recognized with a thump of surprise their own Captain Lewis. With him, they soon learned, rode the commander of the reinforcements, who also proved to be the nephew and secretary of New Mexico's governor. Manuel Chaves had come to offer terms.

Exactly what transpired next is related in the journal of young Franklin Combs, a Kentuckian and, therefore, a citizen of the United States who had come along as a guest of the expedition:

> When Lewis and the governor's nephew and confidential secretary came up, a parley was had between them and the Texians, the troops on both sides maintaining their battle array. Captain Lewis represented the governor as willing to receive the Texians on condition that they would lay down their arms in conformity with the law of Mexico. . . . He represented himself and the nephew and secretary of the governor as empowered to stipulate for the surrender of the implements of war and to negotiate for the safe conduct of the troops to the frontier after they had complied with this stipulation.[6]

Cook and the Texan officers appeared much dismayed with this proposal and not a little suspicious of Captain Lewis' words and actions. The governor's young nephew, who had come unarmed and speaking passable English, made a good impression, but it was Lewis who put the matter on the line when he informed them that Armijo had 3,000 men within twelve hours march. Then, Combs says, "The commissioner, yet not satisfied, Captain Lewis pledged his honor to the truth of all these statements, swearing upon his Masonic faith to every word of it. . . . And not suspecting Lewis to be a traitor, the Texians laid down their arms upon the terms of surrender proposed."[7]

Historians and other writers have generally accepted Combs' verdict that Captain Lewis indeed engaged in betrayal by convincing his former comrades to capitulate when he knew that Armijo would not abide by the terms. It is quite possible, however, that the young officer accepted the governor's words in good faith and honestly believed he meant to treat the Texans well and release them according to his agreement. Certainly from what little is known of the matter, Manuel Chaves seems to have had no inkling that the conditions set before the Texans would not be scrupulously kept, although from sad personal experience he could attest to Armijo's untrustworthiness.[8]

On the day of the surrender, Chaves supplied the ragged and hungry Texans with food, blankets, and the few other provisions that were at his disposal.[9] But according to Combs, such leniency continued only until the following morning when Governor Armijo arrived to take charge with 1,500 men, "a force sufficient to make him secure in his barbarity."[10]

The brief respite from want which the Texans had enjoyed was now abruptly terminated by orders of Armijo.

The prisoners were bound six and eight together with rawhide thongs and hair ropes and placed under heavy guard in a filthy sheep corral. Here they were held for the night, suffering the miseries of close confinement, their limbs pained by the tight ropes. It was now evident that Armijo not only refused to honor the agreement made by his emissaries but was toying with some sinister punishment for the men who had so carelessly fallen under his glove.

A council of all Mexican officers convened in a house adjacent to the corral-prison and throughout the night the Texans listened to a heated dispute over their fate. His Excellency was demanding death for all captives, but even he, with his feigned omnipotence, was not so imprudent as to believe that executing men in violation of the terms of a surrender might not bring down upon his head serious repercussions. Much better to leave the decision to a council of officers, so that any blame could be shifted to others. But this maneuver was easier conceived than carried out, for the proposal was so monstrous that some of Armijo's subordinates, even at the risk of incurring his displeasure, refused to go along. At dawn the debate subsided, the vote was taken, and Armijo lost. By a single ballot, it was decided the prisoners should not be shot but marched off to Mexico City. Young Franklin Combs witnessed the effect of the verdict on the governor who came storming out of the house raving like a madman "because (as we heard) his wish to have us shot had been overruled."[11]

The voice Manuel Chaves raised in this council must be a matter of conjecture. Since, as our narrative will show, he and Armijo crossed swords with regard to military policy at other times, we can safely say that he did not fail to speak his mind on this tense and emotion-filled occasion. And, likewise, since his sympathy and fondness for Anglo-

Americans a few years later is well-documented, and in this instance he had already dealt leniently with the Texans, we may further assume that his vote helped muster the majority of one—for clemency.

Thus spared from death, the prisoners under guard were started on the hard road for Mexico City almost two thousand miles away. A short time later another detachment of Armijo's army commanded by Colonel Juan Andrés Archuleta captured the remainder of the Texans under General McLeod at Laguna Colorado in extreme eastern New Mexico. These too were sent south, in chains, escorted by Captain Salazar who heaped upon them extreme cruelties. Fully aware of the propaganda value of his "victory," Armijo led his triumphant troops to the village of Las Vegas where a great celebration was staged, and proclamations seized from the Texans were publicly burned in the plaza. Retiring to Santa Fe and an enthusiastic reception which awaited him, he wasted no time in firing off letters to the national capital extolling the magnitude of his achievement. In due time his *coup de main* in service to the Republic was accorded official recognition, and on subsequent state occasions the governor was able to sport a large and ostentatious medal, decorated with crossed sabers, and suspended from his bull-like neck by a tri-color ribbon.

According to what Amado Chaves learned from his father long years after the Texan affair, Commissioner William Cook and perhaps several others, after their capture, were taken to Santa Fe for a brief period before being marched to Mexico. Manuel Chaves had become friendly with Cook and by his own request lodged the commissioner in his house in the capital. Cook, by his cordial manner, made many friends, all of whom expressed regret when, under directive of Armijo, he was sent to rejoin those Texans already on the road.[12] With the closing of this episode, Manuel Chaves was left with a new measure of experience and further evidence of the perfidy of his uncle Manuel Armijo.

For the next five years only a few scraps of information have come down to us regarding Manuel's activities. During this period of the early 1840s, according to the recollections of Francisco Perea, young Chaves "built and owned the finest dwelling house in Santa Fe. This structure was built four-square, enclosing a court, and was finished with portals all around outside, and also on the inside bordering the court."[13] This meager description suggests that the residence conformed with the prevailing architectural style in the province—a flat-roofed adobe building; the rooms in line surrounding an open patio, or *placita* as it was generally called in New Mexico; and beamed porches protecting the mud walls from rain and adding to the coolness of interior rooms in summer. Around the edge of the roof ran a brick parapet through which at various points, rain spouts or *canales* projected, giving the appearance of guns aimed from the embrasures of a small fortress.

Behind the house were stables and corrals, since Manuel had not lost his fondness for fine horseflesh. The dwelling itself, according to son Amado, was furnished with articles won from Indians in shooting matches. "While my father lived in Santa Fe," he says, "Indian parties from different parts of the province used to come there for the express purpose of shooting with him, and they would take along horses, blankets, and buckskins to bet. They were invariably defeated."[14] Of this activity, Willa Cather says, "Manuel's house and stables were full of trophies. He took a cool pleasure in stripping the Indians of their horses or silver or blankets, or whatever they had put up on their man.

He was proud of his skill with Indian weapons; he had acquired it in a hard school."[15]

How Manuel Chaves was supporting himself and in such elegant style must be a matter of conjecture. It is known that a few years later he was engaged in various livestock enterprises and was making periodic trading journeys to Chihuahua, so we may surmise that his ability to build, what was for backwoodsy Santa Fe, a true mansion, reflects early successes in these business ventures. Brother Román Baca was again under his care, and perhaps other relatives along with friends and Indian servants composed his household. At Manuel's insistence, Román began his formal education with a private tutor, an old officer of the Mexican army.[16] The boy also may have received instruction in a public school established in 1844 and directed by a highly competent Englishman remembered only as "El Maestro Tatty," who taught the basics of arithmetic, writing, and reading.[17]

The year 1844 serves as a significant benchmark in the life of Manuel Chaves. How long before this he had made the acquaintance of dark-haired María Vicenta Labadie is not known, but since she was a native of the village of Tomé, he must have encountered her on one of his visits to uncle Mariano's hacienda which was in that vicinity. Upon her marriage to Manuel, Vicenta was a tender fifteen.[18] No details of the courtship and wedding have been preserved, but we may assume, since both parties were of good families, that the strict customs regarding such matters were faithfully observed.

As Manuel's father was dead, he probably prevailed upon one of his uncles to deliver the formal document to Vicenta's family requesting her hand. The details were finally arranged by an exchange of letters, and on the appointed day the groom arrived at the Labadie residence in Tomé, accompanied by a suitable entourage of relatives, friends, and servants and bearing a large trunk with the bride's trousseau. The *prendorio* or announcement of the marriage took place and the couple was formally introduced to the assembled crowd. If a private chapel was lacking, the ceremony was conducted in the *sala* (receiving hall), with a priest officiating and musicians of violin and harp producing raucous tunes in the background. After pronouncement of the benediction uniting the couple, guests sought out the refreshment tables bountifully laden with liquors, El Paso wine, and platters of cake and sweetmeats.

If Vicenta Labadie's family roots did not extend quite as far back into New Mexico's soil as those of her new husband, her heritage was a prestigious one nonetheless. Among her ancestors was a Spanish officer, Sebastián Martín Serrano, who was serving in Santa Fe at the end of the seventeenth century.[19] One of his granddaughters, Micaela Padilla, married Domingo Labadie (Dominique L'Abadie?) on November 2, 1766.[20] Labadie was a French physician who reached Santa Fe in 1765 at the age of twenty-seven.[21] Why he left France and under what circumstances he came to New Mexico are unknown. The Labadies produced nine children, one of whom, Pablo, became the father of Manuel's bride. Vicenta, the third child of Pablo Labadie and Rosa Cisneros, had a brother, Lorenzo, and three sisters. Two of the sisters eventually married brothers of Manuel, while Lorenzo wed Rayitos Washington, a grand-niece of the ill-famed Doña Tules, who was also distantly related to Manuel.[22] With each marriage the intricacies of the Chaves family genealogy seemed to proliferate in bewildering complexity.

Portraits made several years after their wedding show

Manuel Antonio Chaves, 1848.

Vicenta Labadie de Chaves, 1848.

Manuel and Vicenta to have been an extraordinarily handsome couple.[23] In her novel *Death Comes for the Archbishop,* Willa Cather draws a picture of Manuel Chaves which was somewhat idealized but probably more truth than fiction. "He was the handsomest man of the company," she writes, "with delicately cut, disdainful features—one had only to see him across the room, or to sit next to him at dinner, to feel the electric quality under his cold reserve; the fierceness of some embitterment, the passion for danger."[24]

From all we know, Manuel's comely features bore the strong stamp of the old Chaves strain. Fray Angélico Chávez, a contemporary historian, recently declared, "Manuel's face was that of my own father as I remember it when he was around forty years old. And he was only my dad's third cousin. But I have noticed the same features on different Chaves males today, which has led me to believe that this is how the original seventeenth century Chaves men looked."[25]

According to descriptions by those who knew him, Manuel was possessed of soft voice; chestnut hair; a fair, almost florid, complexion; steel grey eyes; and a slight, spare frame. He weighed a scant 140 pounds in his prime and stood only five feet, seven inches. Improbable as it may seem, colonial military records indicate that this was about the average height for Spanish soldiers serving in New Mexico. Kit Carson, too, was small of stature and somewhat delicate in appearance, ample confirmation that formidable fighters were not confined to bulky, big-muscled frames.

When Manuel took his bride home to Santa Fe, he was able to offer her not only a fine house but a respected role in the ebullient social life of the capital. A young Englishman, George Frederick Ruxton, who visited the city in 1846, mentioned that "the families of Armijo, Chaves,

Perea, and Ortiz are par excellence the *ricos* or aristocrats of New Mexico."[26] In at least one instance, records testify that Manuel Chaves was among leading citizens who sought to beautify Santa Fe and make needed municipal improvements. It came about in this way.

Mariano Martínez, a native of Mexico who became governor in 1844, looked with some dismay upon the drab streets of his new administrative capital and especially upon the dust-laden public plaza, in front of his palace, which was used indiscriminately as a campground and stockyard. Summoning as advisers those pillars of the community who bore influence, he initiated a program to bring certain amenities to his seat of government. Campers and livestock were cleared from the plaza, and a formidable adobe pyramid surmounted by a flagpole was torn down. This demolition was deemed necessary to preserve public morals, since upon steps of the pyramid gathered idlers and drunks whose displays of impropriety often became the subject of scandal. An observer recorded that this removal aroused considerable discontent among the disorderly element but brought a sigh of relief to sober and peaceable citizens.

Further civic improvement entailed the planting of cottonwood trees and wild flowers throughout the plaza, along principal thoroughfares, and in a park or *alameda* set aside by the governor. Among those mentioned as instrumental in the promotion of this work were Manuel Chaves and Donaciano Vigil, the latter a man who was shortly to play a significant role in New Mexico's political fortunes.[27]

In the late summer of 1844 Governor Martínez was the principal subject in a bizarre incident which, if not directly involving Manuel, at least must have caused a stir within his household, as it did in all others about the capital.

During the last week of August, the governor received disturbing news from the village of Abiquiu, which lay in the Chama Valley about fifty miles northwest of Santa Fe. A large war party of Utes had descended upon that place to complain that New Mexican militiamen had recently attacked their camps and killed ten men in violation of an existing peace between the two peoples. The Indians denounced such treachery and hotly demanded return of four Ute children held captive. They also wanted as compensation for the warriors slain ten horses with bridles and ten serapes. This, they contended, would satisfy them, and they could go away "to forget all their sorrows and remain peaceful forever."[28]

Martínez fired off a letter to the *alcalde* or chief magistrate at Abiquiu directing him to placate the Indians, but a swift reply indicated that the Utes, in an ugly mood, had already started for Santa Fe under their leaders, headed by war chief Panasiyave. On the afternoon of September 5, the governor received the belligerent party, and according to his own words, "placed at their disposal a house for lodging, sheep, bread, and tobacco, along with some other things for their pleasure."[29] The group numbered 108 warriors, including six chiefs.

On the morning following their arrival, the Indians, fairly bristling with weapons, entered the plaza where they refused food that had been prepared for them and angrily threw the governor's gifts into the dust of the street. Indicating a desire to speak with His Excellency, Panasiyave, accompanied by the other chiefs, was led to the palace and ushered into the reception hall near the main entrance. Martínez met them cordially and opened discussions, but it rapidly became apparent the Utes were no longer inclined to be conciliatory. "At this stage," the governor wrote in his official report of the episode, "I ordered them to retire until they reached a decision about what more they should want. I hoped in this way that they would calm themselves."[30]

Far from having a calming effect, the command to leave threw the Utes into an uproar. Panasiyave approached Martínez hurling insults and began pounding him on the chest with his fist. Matters were quickly getting out of hand, as the governor realized when the chief momentarily ceased pummeling and reached up to tweak his beard. At this final indignity, he gave the Indian a forceful shove toward the door, but Panasiyave snatched a war axe from his belt and charged. Martínez grabbed up a chair and brought his assailant to the floor, whereupon the others rushed at him with their arms.

The commotion aroused the governor's wife, who hurried into the room with her husband's sword. Soldiers of the guard were hard on her heels, and for a few seconds a furious battle raged. With Panasiyave dead at their feet, several of the chiefs managed to crash through the window and reach their warriors in the plaza. Here the fighting became more intense as soldiers poured out of their barracks and citizens issued from shops and homes to join the affray. The Utes retreated down San Francisco Street toward the west and as they fled from the outskirts of the city killed several luckless woodcutters who happened to fall in their path. When the turmoil subsided, Governor Martínez, hatless and still gripping his sword, walked through the plaza and surveyed the corpses scattered among the thin saplings of his cottonwoods.[31]

The term of Mariano Martínez as Governor of New Mexico was brief. He came to office early in 1844 by direct appointment of Mexican President Santa Anna, after his predecessor, Manuel Armijo, had resigned claiming ill health. Late the following year, Martínez either quit his post or was removed as a result of questionable handling of customs receipts. With the governorship now vacant, Manuel Armijo, who appears to have effected a quick recovery, jockeyed himself back into his old chair in the capital palace. Leaving his hacienda in Albuquerque, he installed his household in Santa Fe where he fully expected to rule for the next four years, if not longer. But matters of international politics far beyond the control of New Mexicans were fast building to a climax, which within a few months would irrevocably divert the course of the province's history. In the turbulent sweep of events attending the opening of the Mexican War, Governor Armijo would vacate his office for the last time, and young Manuel Chaves would find himself thrust into conflict destined to bring further honor to an already proud family name.

5

Fortunes of War

On December 29, 1845, President James K. Polk formally signed the act annexing the infant Republic of Texas to the United States. Texans, Americans by birth and heritage, had sought admission to the Union as their best security against a threatened reconquest of their land by the armies of Mexico, while expansionist elements in the United States had favored acquisition of Texas as a further step toward pushing the boundaries of the nation to the Pacific. Annexation, however, was not to be accomplished without war, as Polk and his Congress were fully aware, since Mexico clearly had no intention of surrendering claim to her old province. When a Mexican cavalry unit crossed the Rio Grande into Texas on April 24, 1846, and engaged an American patrol, President Polk the following May 13 was led to declare righteously "war exists between the United States and Mexico by the act of the latter."

For many months pro-war sentiment had been growing along the American frontier and in the halls of Congress, fed by the burgeoning spirit of "manifest destiny." Aggressive expansionism had become the mood of the nation, and the call of destiny seemed to demand that the Stars and Stripes be carried to California's shore. Between Texas and California, however, sprawled New Mexico, so expediency and the need for defensible boundaries demanded that that region, too, succumb to conquest. As the *New York Morning News* of August 8, 1846, editorialized, "This territory Mexico has but little interest in retaining, while we have a large one in acquiring it . . . especially if the inhabitants are willing to be transferred to us."[1] The outbreak of the Mexican War thus offered a convenient pretext for achieving the dismemberment of Mexico's northern provinces.

Nowhere was the formal commencement of hostilities more warmly greeted than in the state of Missouri where, because of the long-established Santa Fe trade, New Mexico was already regarded almost as a colonial appendage. But this enthusiasm was tempered by the realization that war inevitably must cause some disruption in commerce. Addressing himself to this problem, the state's influential Senator Thomas Hart Benton urged that guarantees be given to the people of New Mexico "that they shall be protected in all their rights and treated as friends provided they remain quiet and continue trading with us as usual."[2] A more militant note was sounded by the captain of the Laclede Rangers, a company of St. Louis volunteers who had answered the government's call to join an army for the conquest of the Southwest territories. In a rousing speech the officer bellowed, "We shall knock at the gates of Santa Fe as Ethan Allen knocked at the gates of Ticonderoga, and to the question 'Who's there?' we shall reply 'Open these gates in the name of the great Jehovah and the Laclede Rangers.'"[3]

Colonel Stephen Watts Kearny, a veteran of frontier service, was Polk's choice to command the Army of the West, the function of which was to bring about, if possible, a peaceful conquest of New Mexico and California. To do this Kearny had to mollify the residents of Santa Fe and Los Angeles and at the same time hold his obstreperous Missouri boys in check, neither of these an easy undertaking. When the troops, among them the Laclede Rangers, assembled at Fort Leavenworth in the spring of 1846, they numbered 1,600 soldiers, certainly an unimposing force to march through half a continent.

During the last week of June, Albert Speyer, accompanying a Missouri caravan, arrived in Santa Fe and proceeded straight to the Palace of the Governor for a meeting with His Excellency Manuel Armijo. Speyer, a Prussian Jew in partnership with Armijo for several years, had carried goods from the United States to markets in New Mexico and Chihuahua. The news that he bore of Kearny's advance across the plains proved most disconcerting to the governor, who in short order prevailed upon his partner to buy out his interest in their business. At the same time that he quietly began liquidation of other enterprises, Armijo issued a fervent proclamation to his subjects and to the provincial assembly calling upon all citizens to be prepared to render "reserveless sacrifices" as the forces of the United States were moving against New Mexico.

About August 9 the governor convened a council of representative leaders to discuss the approaching crisis. Even the meager accounts available suggest that this was a stormy session. The majority of the participants were already overawed by exaggerated rumors concerning the size and strength of the invading army, and they meekly urged surrender. But the priests opposed submission and with considerable asperity fulminated against the Americans,

General Stephen Watts Kearny, Commander of the Army of the West. *Courtesy Museum of New Mexico.*

whom they claimed would stable their mules in the churches, debauch Catholic women, and pillage the town. Less intemperate in their rhetoric than the priests but no less determined in their patriotism were several young men, among them Manuel Chaves and Miguel Pino of the militia, and Colonel Diego Archuleta of the regular garrison and Armijo's second in command, who formed a loud minority demanding a dedicated defense of the homeland. It is plain from the beginning that Armijo had no stomach for a fight and was openly hostile to the war faction. According to a statement made by Santa Fe refugee Mariano Barela to Mexican authorities after he had fled to Chihuahua, the governor would have taken no measures for defense had not Commandants Chaves and Pino threatened to shoot him. Thus intimidated he announced his readiness to oppose the invasion and with frantic motions initiated measures to rally the New Mexicans.[4]

Five days after the council meeting, upon being advised by his scouts of the presence of Kearny's command near the eastern frontier, Governor Armijo sent a letter to his adversary warning grandiloquently that "the people of the country have risen en masse in my defense, and if you take the province it will be because you prove stronger in battle."[5] At the same time he issued appeals to his subjects to "repel the Americans who are coming to invade our soil and destroy our properties and liberties." Some overzealous persons in Santa Fe whispered that the Missouri merchants living in the town should be killed to prevent them from offering aid or information to the enemy, but Armijo, to his credit, put a stop to such talk.

By August 14 the governor had mustered the forces available for New Mexico's preservation: three companies of regular presidial troops, a small relief detachment recently arrived from Mexico, a motley assortment of militiamen numbering perhaps 2,000, and a battery of artillery composed of six cannon. On the following morning, Armijo, heralded by a grand flourish of trumpets and rolling of drums, mounted a horse in front of the mud palace and with the army at his back swung out on the broadly marked trail leading east. With some apprehension the residents of Santa Fe watched the departure of the soldiers, for Armijo's lack of true generalship was too well known to inspire confidence among those who now looked to him for protection.

The governor had selected a natural defensive position about ten miles east of the capital to make his stand. Here the Santa Fe Trail passed through the narrow jaws of Apache Canyon, which at its mouth was only wide enough for a single wagon to pass. Placing the cannon on a small hill just outside the defile and throwing up crude breastworks of earth and timber, the New Mexicans gave all appearances of preparation for battle. But already their will to fight was beginning to crumble. Militia officers Manuel Chaves and Miguel Pino went among the poorly armed men endeavoring to inflame their patriotism and will to resist, but their efforts were largely nullified by Governor Armijo whose lack of enthusiasm for the whole enterprise was becoming apparent to all. The governor, in fact, before leaving Santa Fe, had privately cleaned up the last of his affairs and granted power of attorney to one of his associates, indicating he did not expect to return. When his officers realized that the move to Apache Pass was all for show, they called Armijo to account. But with feigned resignation, he declared that Kearny's army by his reports was too strong and that to avoid bloodshed he intended to dissolve the militia.

Colonel Pino, supported by his friend Manuel Chaves, expressed his determination to uphold New Mexico's honor and offered to attack the enemy if he could have part of the regular troops. Armijo adamantly refused, whereupon some of his staff uttered threats and called him a traitor. This so aroused the governor's ire that he turned the cannon toward his own forces and ordered the militiamen to disband and return to their homes. Seeing that the army was a shambles, the officers dismissed their troops, leaving Armijo only in command of the regular presidial companies. Chaves and Pino, following in the wake of the fleeing militia, hastened toward Santa Fe to look to the protection of their families. But the governor, with full realization that his chapter in New Mexico's history had closed, fled south toward Chihuahua. Whether his lack of action at Apache Canyon was dictated by sobriety of judgment or simple cowardice is still a matter of debate.[6]

In Santa Fe meanwhile all was pandemonium. Shortly after Armijo's departure with the army, wild rumors spread that he had been assassinated by his men and that the small contingent of troops from Mexico, a rowdy undisciplined lot, was returning to massacre the American merchants and plunder their stores. Upon heels of this, the first of the militia came hurrying in with the news that the governor, not dead at all, had abandoned his government and people to their fate and that Kearny's army was fast approaching the limits of the town.

Members of the Santa Fe municipal council met in urgent session and gravely discussed the propriety of tearing down the churches to prevent their being profaned and turned into barracks. But several Americans came forward with assurances that their countrymen were not so callous as to desecrate places of worship, and the churches were spared.[7]

At the same time, many respectable people of the town were joining an exodus into the countryside "to hide themselves in the desert" and save their wives and daughters from dishonor. Upon word that Armijo had deserted, a solid and fearless citizen, Juan Bautista Vigil y Alarid, assumed the acting-governorship and exerted efforts to allay the fears of the populace. In public places he posted copies of a proclamation sent ahead by Kearny promising to respect the religion and property of the New Mexicans. Since Manuel Chaves was thoroughly familiar with the Americans, we cannot suppose that he lent himself to the general panic. More likely he joined with Vigil y Alarid and other cooler heads urging calm and probably assured his wife Vicenta that no mass assault upon Santa Fe womanhood would ensue with the impending occupation.

About five o'clock on the afternoon of August 18, the Army of the West rumbled into the narrow streets of the capital. General Kearny, who had received his promotion from colonel en route to New Mexico, led the dragoons in the van, followed by the infantry, while the artillery took up a position on a hill southeast of the town. Curious children trailed in awe behind the glittering cavalcade, while somber men and dark-eyed women, some of them sobbing, observed from behind latticed windows the passing of the troops. In the plaza Kearny and members of his staff dismounted and entered the ancient Palace of the Governors, where they were formally and courteously met by acting-governor Vigil y Alarid and a score of prominent Santa Feans. If Chaves was among those receiving the conquerors, we have no record of it. Glasses of El Paso wine and brandy were passed around, and while all sipped in an atmosphere of cordiality, the troops outside hoisted the Stars and Stripes over the Palace and administered a salute of thirteen guns.

The historic Spanish Governor's Palace on the plaza in Santa Fe. *Parkhurst photo, courtesy Museum of New Mexico.*

For the first time in their history, the Americans had taken a foreign capital, and the conquest had been made without firing a shot.

During the weeks that followed, General Kearny took measures to consolidate his hold on New Mexico. A provisional territorial government was organized with Charles Bent, a respected trader, as governor, and Donaciano Vigil, representative of an eminent local family, serving as secretary. A new legal code was promulgated to supplant the laws of Mexico, a fort was begun on heights commanding the plaza, and various expeditions were dispatched throughout the province to receive the submission of both New Mexicans and Indians. The soldiers, after their tiresome march across the plains, reveled in the pleasures offered by Santa Fe—liquor and gaming tables in the cantinas; weekly fandangos; fresh fruits, meat, and piquant stews seasoned with chili peppers. Some of the more imaginative troopers, among them members of the Laclede Rangers, formed a theatrical company and offered to the public the stirring tragedy of *Barbarossa,* the farce *Fortune's Frolic,* with gentlemen taking the ladies' parts, and the *Virginia Minstrels* singing "The Old Colored Gentleman," "Blue Tail Fly," and "You Ain't Good Looking and You Can't Come In."[8]

Believing the conquest of New Mexico complete, the ambitious Kearny was eager to be on his way to California where awaited further opportunities to add luster to his name. Late in September he started west with the main army, leaving a respectable force in Santa Fe to garrison the newly won territory. Colonel Sterling Price, in command of these troops, soon found that his men, most of them undisciplined volunteers, were growing troublesome because of the idleness attendant upon garrison duty, and incidents of drunken street brawling became of daily concern.

Meantime, many New Mexicans remained inwardly unreconciled to alien rule, and their resentment increased as the loud, arrogant Americans swaggered through the streets of their capital. Probably soon after Kearny's departure had reduced the number of foreign soldiers, quiet talk began concerning the possibilities of fomenting a rebellion. Leaders among the conspirators came from the clergy and the old ruling families who understood the changes in local institutions and society that must inevitably follow the imposition of a new order. At a series of secret meetings, some of them held in a house on the plaza opposite the old Palace, various plans were discussed and then abandoned as unworkable. Privy to these discussions were Manuel Chaves; Miguel Pino and his older brother Nicolás; the brother of the ecclesiastical vicar of Santa Fe, Tomás Ortiz; Armijo's old subordinate, Diego Archuleta; and a dozen others, including several priests.[9] It rapidly became evident that some of the plotters, chiefly Ortiz and Archuleta, desired to promote a general uprising which would result in a massacre of all Americans. As later events would indicate, Chaves and the Pinos spoke out against unbridled bloodshed, and when they could not carry the others with their arguments for moderation became lukewarm to the intrigue.

Those who remained wedded to violence set the nineteenth of December as the day for rising, and Vicar Juan Felipe Ortiz and Padre José Manuel Gallegos went into the rural districts to win adherents from among the farming folk. The intent was to seize the leaders of government and American military commanders and in their place install Tomás Ortiz as governor and Diego Archuleta as commandant general of the revolutionary forces. Because of delays in organization, the blow was delayed until midnight Christmas Eve when, it was felt, the soldiers would be off guard and could be easily overcome. The sound of the church bell was to be the signal for attack, and the artillery was to be captured first so it could be turned into the streets.[10]

All the plans went awry, however. Several days before Christmas, Colonel Price got word of what was afoot and took immediate steps to arrest the ringleaders and nip the conspiracy in the bud. A popular story holds that Doña Tules, who had ingratiated herself with the handsome foreign officers, learned details of the plot from gossips in her gambling hall and conveyed the news to Secretary Vigil who was strongly pro-American.[11] Diego Archuleta slipped out of the city and escaped, as did Tomás Ortiz, who disguised himself as a woman and, carrying a water jar on his head, walked past a patrol of soliders to a thicket along the Santa Fe River where his horse was tied.

According to a hasty investigation conducted by Colonel Price, Manuel Chaves and the Pino brothers were implicated in the affair, and they were shortly arrested while sitting under the portal of the old Exchange Hotel (today the famous La Fonda). Certain persons of influence suggested that Chaves be shot immediately, as he was the most dangerous fighter of the trio and his death would handily serve to intimidate others who might be contemplating resistance. But Price had no intention of circumventing proper legal procedure, since he wished to demonstrate the equability of the American system of justice.[12]

The accused were lodged in the *calabozo* or jail located in the west end of the Governor's Palace, while Colonel Price began looking into their activities more closely. The Pinos, he found, were highly regarded in the community, being the sons of the late Don Pedro Bautista Pino, the only man ever to represent New Mexico in the Spanish parliament. Since the evidence against the brothers seemed thin, he ordered their release. But about the conduct of Manuel Chaves he still held some reservations, so he sent Captain William Angney to interrogate the prisoner in his cell. The Captain sought to discover if Manuel was in sympathy with the movement and if he could be trusted should he be returned to freedom. To this Chaves replied:

> Captain, be kind enough to take my compliments to Colonel Price and say that he has nothing to fear from me now. When Armijo disbanded the volunteers at Cañoncito [Apache Pass], I gave up all hope of being any service to my country at this time, and my record as a man will show that I am not at all likely to sympathize with any movement to murder people in cold blood. Tell him also that if the time ever comes when I can be of any service to my own country, Colonel Price will find me in the front ranks.[13]

In spite of this straightforward speech, Manuel remained in custody, and preparations were made to bring him to trial before a military court. At this point the records make vague allusions to "his enemies" who gained the ear of Price and having failed to see Chaves shot, now took care to summon whatever might be contrived in the way of evidence to damage him before the court. The identity of these enemies remains a mystery, but they or others, like elusive shadows, appeared at later moments in his career and on at least one occasion threatened the life of his eldest son. Certainly Manuel Chaves was a strong personality, as his story to this point unmistakably reveals, and some affair of honor or some business matter may have earned him the undying enmity of powerful foes. But of this we unfortunately have no information.

One amusing incident occurred while Manuel was detained in the *calabozo* awaiting trial. Since the lock-up did not furnish meals to prisoners, those held were dependent upon relatives or friends for this service. Young Román Baca assumed the task of carrying food to his brother and in a short time became friendly with the good-natured guards. Entering the jail one evening with his laden tray, Román found a new soldier on duty who, perhaps filled with his own self-importance, insisted on a meticulous examination of the food, even breaking open the biscuits. Infuriated over this indignity, Román flung the dishes into the man's face and then, aghast at his own rashness, fled with the laughter of the remaining guards ringing in his ears.[14]

Captain Angney, who had been a Missouri lawyer before assuming command of two infantry companies in Kearny's army, was selected to defend Chaves.[15] During the second week of January, 1847, the defendant was taken before a board of military officers and informed that the charge against him was treason. This seems to have been based upon a blanket declaration made by General Kearny when he first entered the territory that New Mexicans, henceforward, would be regarded as United States citizens and any who rebelled would be considered traitors. The position, of course, was of dubious legality, since the war with Mexico was still in progress and the status of residents in the conquered provinces yet to be determined by Congress.

This was recognized by the highly competent Angney, and in an eloquent defense before the military tribunal he pointed out that Manuel Chaves, in fact, was still a citizen of Mexico, that whatever activity he had been engaged in was in defense of his government, and that far from guilty of treason, he was worthy of commendation as a patriot. With emotion the captain declared that Chaves deserved "the admiration of all brave men" and that the United States "would forever bear the stain of disgrace if it undertook under any pretext to shoot a man for endeavoring to defend his country in time of need."[16] The court was moved by both the plea and the soundness of the argument, and Manuel Chaves was acquitted and released immediately. Retiring to his home, he was greeted by Vicenta and friends who had spent several anxious weeks awaiting his fate.

The rebellion against American occupation, stillborn in Santa Fe, was far from dead outside the capital. To the north in Taos, always a seedbed of discontent, other rebels took up the cudgel and laid plans to challenge the new lords of the land. Involved in this activity were Mexican residents of the village of Don Fernando de Taos, as well as Indians of nearby Taos Pueblo who possessed a long history of opposition to established authority. On January 5, Governor Bent issued a stern proclamation condemning the abortive plot in Santa Fe and warning against future acts of treachery.[17] Two weeks later, discounting reports that the north was still boiling, the governor improvidently journeyed to Taos where he had long maintained his home and had many friends. On the morning of January 19, he was set upon by a howling mob and scalped alive before the horrified eyes of his wife and children. Other supporters of American rule at nearby Arroyo Hondo and at Mora eastward beyond the mountains were also slain. So, after all, the fate of New Mexico was not to be decided without a bloodletting.

With the success of the revolt in Taos, rebel emissaries were sent to the capital in an effort to rekindle the fire there, but Sterling Price (recently promoted to brigadier-general) took prompt steps to prepare his defenses. According to messages from the seat of rebellion, 1,500 Mexicans and Indians were advancing against Santa Fe, while Price had only 300 troops under his command. To bolster his forces, he summoned renowned mountain man Ceran St. Vrain and prevailed upon him to recruit a company of volunteers. St. Vrain, born near St. Louis, had embarked in the fur trade as a youth and appeared in Taos as early as 1825. Several years later he formed a partnership with Charles Bent under the name Bent, St. Vrain & Company, which lasted until Bent's assassination.[18] Thus St. Vrain was a logical choice to lead the volunteers in avenging the death of his close friend and partner.

In a brief period St. Vrain, who had received a commission as captain, rounded up sixty-five willing recruits, most of them trappers and traders. For reasons of his own, he approached several New Mexicans and extended them an invitation to join. Among those who responded were Nicolás Pino and Manuel Chaves. Apparently St. Vrain was already an admirer of Manuel and aware of the young man's reputation as a scrappy fighter when he visited his home only a few days after the trial and proffered him an officer's appointment in the new "Emergency Brigade." Chaves agreed to enroll but declined to accept the commission, perhaps because, as one writer has stated, it might have irritated the Americans.[19] Thus, after taking a formal oath of allegiance to the United States, Chaves entered service as a private, and his friend Nicolás Pino followed suit.[20] The muster roll for the new company shows that on January 23, 1847, Manuel Chaves, age twenty-six, enlisted for "duration of the revolution" with one horse valued at $65.00 and saddle and tack worth $16.00.[21]

After assessing his situation, General Price decided as a bold gamble to take the offensive. This meant leaving Santa Fe undefended and moving out with an army that, except

Colonel Ceran St. Vrain, mountain man, Santa Fe trader, and friend of Manuel Chaves, who served under him at the Battle of Taos in 1847 and again during the Ute-Jicarilla War in 1855. *Courtesy Museum of New Mexico.*

for the volunteers, was unmounted. Nevertheless, these disadvantages seemed outweighed by the perils of inaction which could only accrue to the benefit of the enemy. Therefore, with his troops and a battery of four twelve-pounder mountain howitzers, he pushed north twenty miles to the village of La Cañada where the first engagement of the campaign was fought. Here, athwart the main road, the Taos rebels had taken possession of several low hills and three strongly fortified adobe houses at their base. Price drew up his battle line with the artillery guarding the left flank and the companies under Captain Angney prepared to make a frontal assault. Amidst the maneuvering, a detachment of Mexicans slipped behind the American position and attacked the supply train, but St. Vrain's volunteers fell back and drove them off. In this Manuel Chaves saw his first action in defense of the government he had so recently acknowledged. The enemy, more of an unorganized, ragtag mob than an army, soon gave way in the face of a direct charge and retreated toward the north, leaving La Cañada to the victors.

Hastening in pursuit, the inspirited Americans slogged up the canyon of the Rio Grande through deep snow, shielding their faces from a bitter winter gale that swept off the high peaks of the Sangre de Cristos. Near Embudo the trail was pinched between steep walls of a canyon and here in the last defensible position before Taos, the insurgents again rallied for a stand. Their men were arrayed on both walls of the gorge where broken lava and a heavy growth of juniper provided excellent protection. According to General Price's official report, "The action was commenced by Captain St. Vrain, who dismounting his men, ascended the mountain on the left, doing much execution."[22] Captain Burgwin forced the line on the canyon floor and with the aid of flanking parties routed the defenders from the pass. With this the road to Taos was clear, and Price and his men marched swiftly toward the climax of their campaign.

The rebels had elected to fortify the Indian pueblo, which according to General Price was "a place of great strength being surrounded by adobe walls and strong pickets." Within the enclosure were two large multi-storied mud dwellings and a thick-walled church, all provided with loop-holes for rifles. In mid-afternoon of February 3, the artillery unleashed a two-hour barrage against the stout walls, but the cannon balls bounced off harmlessly as the defenders jeered. At nightfall the soldiers retired to the adjacent town of Fernando de Taos, but on the morrow Price had his men back in position and by nine o'clock he was ready to take the pueblo by storm. He says, "I ordered the mounted men under Captains St. Vrain and Slack [the latter had joined the army with reinforcements en route to Taos] to a position on the opposite side of the town, whence they could discover and intercept any fugitives who might attempt to escape toward the mountains, or in the direction of Don Fernando."[23] In the fierce battle that followed, gallant Captain Burgwin under a withering fire led a rush against the western wall of the church, and though he fell mortally wounded, his men breached the defenses and fired the roof of the building. Captain Angney with his infantry companies assailed the pueblo dwelling routing Mexicans, Taos Indians, and a handful of their Apache allies. Many of these fled toward the mountains but were pursued by the mounted volunteers under Captain St. Vrain who killed fifty-one.[24]

It was in this part of the melee that Manuel Chaves saved his commanding officer and demonstrated that St. Vrain's

Taos Pueblo. Assaulted by American forces after the revolt of 1847. *New Mexico Department of Development photo.*

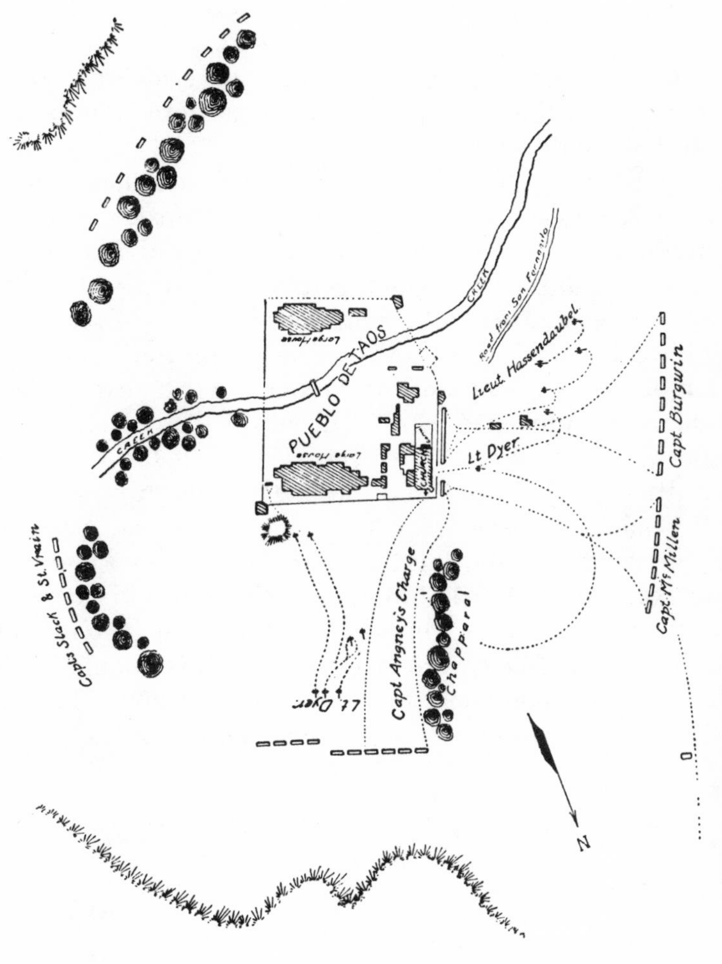

Map of the Battle of Taos, February 3-4, 1847.

trust had not been misplaced. The two men were fighting side by side as the fleeing rebels passed through their lines. Manuel had just emptied his Hawkins rifle when he saw a burly Apache leap from the brush and drag the Captain from his horse. The pair grappled furiously in the snow with St. Vrain straining desperately to hold back a knife aimed at his chest. Manuel bounded in and laid the barrel of his empty weapon smartly across the warrior's head, fracturing his skull. As he dragged the body off St. Vrain, his commander was gasping for breath but grinning. When Manuel grinned back, a friendship was born that lasted the rest of their lives.[25]

Success at the battle of Taos effectively quelled opposition to American sovereignty over New Mexico. Manuel returned to his wife and home in Santa Fe and, like others of his kind, began putting together the pieces of a life that had been so recently shattered. Secretary Donaciano Vigil had become acting-governor of the territory upon the death of Charles Bent, but for the next several years virtual military rule prevailed, since real power was exercised by a succession of commanding generals. With the fading of civil disorder, the problem of raiding Navajo, Apache, Ute, and Comanche became of uppermost concern, both to territorial officials and the common citizenry who bore the brunt of Indian attacks. Manuel Chaves would soon be drawn into the storm whipped up by new wars with the Indians, but first he was to enjoy a respite that would allow him to put his household in some order and give attention to business interests necessary for the support of his family.

6
Interlude

On the front page of the *Santa Fe Republican* for May 31, 1848, appeared the following announcement of general interest to the public:

NOTICE

Good grazing for all kinds of stock,
At the very low price of
ONE DOLLAR & 50 cts., per month!!!

Notice is hereby given that the undersigned is now prepared to take in any amount of stock to feed, at the very low price of one dollar and fifty cents per month, a head, for any kind of stock.

He would also inform the public that his pastures and grazing grounds are large, and supplied with good watering privileges, and the best quality of grass, and plenty of it. No pains will be spared in attending to the stock that should be entrusted to his care. He has many hands, and they are all well armed so as to defend the stock from the Indians.

> He holds himself responsible for all stock entrusted to his keeping (death and accident excepted) unless it should be run off by the Indians, of which there is little or no danger, as he is well provided with arms and herders, and he has large and commodious corrals for them at night if necessary.
>
> All persons wishing their stock to be sent out immediately, will please call on Mr. James Giddings, who will receive them and send them to the grazing camp.
>
> The subscribers pastures are only twenty or thirty miles from this city, in the vicinity of Galisteo.
>
> MANUEL CHAVES
>
> References, Hon. Joab Houghton, Chas. Blumner, O.P. Hovey, Abell & Duvall, Wm. S. Smith, J.M. Giddings, and all the Americans who have lived in Santa Fe any length of time.
>
> Santa Fe, May 30, 1848.

The year and a half in Manuel's history from the battle of Taos to the appearance of this notice is a vacuum, but the details of the advertisement demonstrate that he had not been idle. With the same assiduousness that he had once organized woodcutters in St. Louis, he had in Santa Fe, as soon as some degree of normalcy had returned to New Mexico, set about establishing a livestock business of considerable magnitude. His attention to detail—the large and commodious corrals for handling cattle and horses and the formidable array of armed guards—tell something of his business acumen and the sense of responsibility he felt toward those who placed their stock in his charge. Nor does the fact that he claims the confidence of "all Americans who have lived in Santa Fe any length of time" fail to impress. The ones he names, including Judge Joab Houghton, were among the civic and commercial leaders of the community.

It is apparent from Manuel's statement that the American military presence in New Mexico had, within a short time, greatly reduced the Indian menace in the vicinity of Santa Fe. The Galisteo Basin southeast of the town, which Manuel intended to graze, had long served as an avenue for Plains raiders in their descent upon the Rio Grande settlements. In late colonial times, the horse herd of the royal presidial garrison had found pasturage there on rolling plains carpeted with grama and wheat grass, but incessant thefts by hostile nomads had made use of this range extremely risky. Nor did conditions improve under the succession of Mexican governors prior to 1846. When Kearny cut his swath across New Mexico, however, he served notice to the Indian tribes that depredations would not be tolerated and that troops aplenty would be maintained to enforce the peace. These blandishments had small effect, but for several years after the conquest American soldiery did provide a measure of safety for the precincts close to Santa Fe.

In 1849 a daughter, Perfilia, was born to Manuel and Vicenta Chaves, their first child.[1] The following year the family moved into a new house located immediately behind the chapel of Guadalupe on Santa Fe's west side. That Manuel gave a mere $150 for the dwelling[2] suggests that his livestock venture had not paid off and that he had suffered reverses in whatever other business he was engaged, obliging him to dispose of the large residence he had maintained during the 1840s. By mid-century Indians were becoming troublesome again, and anyone with investments in commercial vehicles on the road or stock on the open range could find himself in financial difficulties as a result of a single devastating raid. That Manuel was personally concerned with the Indian problem at this time is evidenced by his taking the lead in the organization of six companies of volunteers to go and fight hostile Navajos, about which more will be said shortly.

Although the Chaves house in Guadalupe parish was modest in size, it enjoyed a pleasant and convenient location. Along the north side of the property flowed a sparkling stream, pretentiously called the Santa Fe River. Fruit trees and cottonwoods shaded the banks, and a patchwork of tiny garden plots drank from the *acequias* that funneled off the waters from the principal stream. Below the Chaves house was the sprawling hacienda-like home of Donaciano Vigil, perched on a bank above the river, while directly to the south the old Camino Real, the main thoroughfare from Albuquerque and El Paso, threaded its way through the Guadalupe suburb en route to the capital's main plaza.

Manuel Chaves, like all those of Spanish descent, looked forward to a male heir who could one day shoulder the patriarchal responsibilities of the family name. On April 16, 1851, a son, Amado, was born in the house by the Santa Fe River, and a short time afterward, on the 30th of that month, the proud father presented him for baptism. His good friend Don Miguel Pino, with whom he had been involved in the conspiracy of 1846, was asked to stand as godfather.[3]

At about this same period Manuel began to develop the close relationship with Lorenzo Labadie, his brother-in-law, that would soon blossom into a firm business partnership.[4] Lorenzo, several years the junior, was a handsome and extremely affable young man who held strong admiration for his sister's husband. In May of 1852 Manuel posted bond on his behalf before the United States Indian agent so that he could secure a license to trade with the Navajo for a period of three months. Lorenzo, as his later record reveals, had an easy way with Indians, and his straightforward manner invariably won their trust. In this instance, he probably carried not only his own trade goods, but those of his sponsoring kinsman. At this time Manuel also applied for a license to open commercial activity with the southern Apaches, but as these people had recently committed a number of depredations, the military authorities were contemplating a campaign against them, and the request was denied.[5]

These small pieces of information confirm that Manuel Chaves was involved in the Indian trade, although probably on no large scale. That he was also engaged in commercial traffic with Mexico during these years was attested to by Amado who recalled much later that his father had made many trips to Chihuahua where he purchased bolts of broadcloth and velvet and brought them home to be made into fine clothes by local tailors.[6] This affinity for the merchant's life Manuel must have acquired in youth from his uncles Mariano and Antonio José, both of whom were now dead. But his father, Julián, had been a cattle and sheep man, and in the end it was to ranching that he felt the strongest pull.

In the early 1850s Manuel and Lorenzo took up lands along the fertile valley of the Pecos River thirty leagues or more east of Santa Fe. Initially their pastures seem to have been leased in the vicinity of the village of San Miguel and stocked only with sheep, but as time went on they acquired more property extending south to the vicinity of Puerto de Luna and the famous cottonwood grove called Bosque Redondo, where a few years later the Navajo and Mescalero Apache would be held in captivity. The details now available lead us to believe that ranching on the Pecos in this troublous period was filled with peril and hardship and that profits, owing to the Indian danger, were even more elusive than was the usual case in such endeavor. John Greiner, senior Indian agent in New Mexico, in his official report of May 21, 1852, noted that the Jicarilla Apache had killed six sheep and all the dogs of the shepherds in an assault upon the Bosque Redondo. The stock, he declared, was owned by Manuel Chaves.[7] Two months later he mentioned receiving word that more sheep belonging to Chaves had been run off, but this story proved to be untrue. Nevertheless, Manuel was having his problems.

In the years after 1851, the Santa Fe house continued to shelter the growing Chaves family, while Manuel was absent for prolonged spells, attending to his precarious ranching affairs in the Pecos valley, making a sheep drive to California in 1852, and participating in an increasing number of Indian campaigns.[8] Young Amado soon had a brother, Irineo, and with their older sister, Perfilia, the boys played along the sandy margin of the Santa Fe stream. Their chaperon-tutor was José Manuel Armenta, nicknamed *El Corona,* who had been in the employ of Manuel since the early 1840s. Armenta was rich in knowledge of the history and folklore of New Mexico, and in the heat of a summer's afternoon, gathering the youngsters under a canopy of cottonwood shade, he spun stories of the Spanish conquest and the long years of unremitting warfare with the Indians. And he imparted to his eager listeners the treasure trove of folksayings, riddles, and tales that formed the heritage of every New Mexican child.[9]

In 1854 Manuel Chaves joined with Lorenzo Labadie in borrowing from Miguel Pino the sum of $6,200, to be repaid within a year at 6 percent interest. For what business purpose the pair planned to use the money is not ascertainable, but the property, both personal and real estate, they put up as security against the loan is of some interest in itself.

The Chaves house in Santa Fe was included in the mortgage deed along with some of its furnishings and several of Manuel's personal articles, all of which serve as evidence of his relative affluence. The enumeration, in addition to the house, went as follows: eight yoke of oxen, two buckskin mules, one dark mule, one burro, one thin horse, one gaited gray mare, one cart with two horses, two large carts, one wagon with three sets of harness, two fine rifles, three pistols with cylinders, two horse-hair sofas, six large mirrors in brackets, two fine chests of drawers, four large chests, one bedstead, four rugs of American fiber, four picture prints, three candelabras of crystal, two silver candelabras, and two hundred assorted vigas (roof beams).

Lorenzo's contribution consisted of a ruined house of four rooms that faced the public plaza in his native village of Tomé, a vineyard, a tract of land north of Tomé on which two mills were located, and a rancho called Ojuelos. Personal property included five horses, a well-broken mule, a pistol, and a rifle.[10] Mention of the Ojuelos Ranch is interesting, for there beneath the shadow of the Manzano Mountains, Manuel would soon move his family. Presumably, the debt to Pino was paid off within the required time, since both Chaves and Labadie continued in possession of their property.

One final incident of some note is remembered for the last period of Manuel's residence in Santa Fe, and it concerns an altercation with the powerful and austere Bishop of New Mexico, John B. Lamy. Although raised in a Catholic household, Manuel, like many Spanish males, was not an ardent churchgoer. During his Indian fighting days, he

Gold medal of the Virgin of Guadalupe carried by Manuel Chaves during his Indian campaigns. *Bart Durham photo.*

always carried a gold medal bearing the likeness of the Virgin of Guadalupe, but this was no real indicator of reliance upon Divine Providence, since as trader Josiah Gregg mentions in the 1840s, "Similar medals are worn by nearly nine-tenths of the population of northern Mexico."[11] In whatever ways Manuel may have been remiss in attention to formal religion, ample compensation was provided by his pious wife Vicenta who carefully saw that their children observed all the requirements of the Church.

The date cannot be fixed with certainty, but most likely sometime in the late 1850s Manuel began to have serious problems regarding the east boundary dividing his land from that of Guadalupe Chapel. Property limits in this period, owing to a dearth of surveyors, were rather vaguely defined, and disputes between neighbors were common. Manuel's case was complicated by the fact that in his dispute he had to contend with the formidable power of the Church, and the awesome ecclesiastical establishment was not accustomed to losing arguments.

Manuel Chaves, however, was never one to be intimidated, and so, over the protests of his wife, he took the offensive. Assembling several wagon loads of cedar pickets and calling out his servants, he threw up a stout fence to separate his house from the chapel and encompass the land he regarded as his own. The priest of Guadalupe was appalled by the rashness of this act and the affront it offered to the Church, and when his protests had no effect, he hastened to the cathedral near the main plaza to lay the matter before Bishop Lamy. His Excellency sent a swift summons to Manuel, and when the young offender appeared, a heated exchange ensued.

"You have encroached upon lands of the Church," thundered the Bishop.

Archbishop John B. Lamy of Santa Fe. *Courtesy Museum of New Mexico.*

"I have fenced what is legally mine," retorted Manuel.

"You will remove the offending barrier."

"I will not!"

"You will comply under pain of excommunication."

And a final burst from Manuel, "The fence remains, and you will not excommunicate me. It would break my poor wife's heart." And he stalked from the interview.

In some anger Bishop Lamy took up pen and parchment and prepared the document expelling Manuel Chaves from the Church. This he dispatched to Guadalupe parish so the pronouncement of doom might be read from the pulpit and thereby rendered official. What consternation this impending order caused in the Chaves home we can well imagine. Not only were there the tearful pleadings of Vicenta, but a parade of friends urged Manuel to back down, to relent, to demolish the fence. But through all he remained immutable.

The following Sunday, Guadalupe Chapel was packed, only a bench-like pew at the front standing vacant. As the service began, a shuffling at the door caused all heads to strain in that direction. Manuel Chaves, chin held high, strode down the center aisle, trailed by Román Baca and a servant. All three were conspicuously armed with rifles, and with considerable aplomb they seated themselves on the empty bench. The priest, after a momentary faltering, went on with the service, but from time to time cast nervous glances toward the front of his congregation. When the point arrived for announcements and the sermon, he mounted the pulpit on shaky legs and extracted an impressive roll of parchment from his sleeve. As he did, the three men below cocked back the hammers on the rifles lying on their laps, the noise echoing through the cavernous length of the chapel.

This menacing gesture was quite sufficient to deter the good Father from reading announcements, or for that matter from delivering sermons, and without another word, he descended from his perch and went on with the service. At the conclusion, Manuel led the retreat of his men back up the aisle, and for the last time in his life he passed out the doors of Guadalupe Chapel. But the order of excommunication was never read.[12]

7

Indian Fighter

In 1851 Manuel Chaves, then in his early thirties, began to take an active part in a growing number of military campaigns being waged against hostile Indians infesting New Mexico's frontier on all sides. Before the decade was out, his fights with Utes and Jicarilla Apaches in the north, Navajos in the west, and various bands of the Gila Apaches in the south were already making his name something of a legend throughout the territory. In the beginning he often came forward to volunteer his arms, but as his reputation grew, more and more American army commanders or New Mexican citizens who had lost property to raiders sought out his services as a scout or leader of punitive expeditions. Manuel's deft coolness under fire, his familiarity with Indian ways and especially with their tactics of war, and his knowledge of terrain and trails preeminently qualified him as one of the finest New Mexican campaigners of this period.

The first planned operation under the leadership of

Manuel Chaves about which we have any record was an expedition against the Navajos in the late spring of 1851. Several incidents of the previous months serve to explain his motives in singling out these Indians for punishment. From about mid-1850 onward, Navajo raids with increasing frequency plagued the settlers of northern New Mexico; the new civil governor, James S. Calhoun, lamented almost daily the army's inability to provide protection. For example, on June 20 a war party of Navajos struck along the Rio Puerco not far from Cebolleta and ran off stock belonging to José Antonio Chávez, Felipe Herrera, and other ranchers. Francisco Chaves, probably a cousin of Manuel's, gathered a handful of men and started in pursuit; but, upon overtaking the raiders, the men found themselves vastly outnumbered and were forced to retreat, suffering five wounded, including Francisco, and the loss of five saddle mules. The Cebolletans experienced similar attacks throughout that summer and fall, one of the worst occurring in October at a sheep camp called Agua Salada, where the Indians stole a flock numbering 3,869 animals and killed two shepherds.[1]

Not long after this incident, the Navajos fell upon Valverde Ranch on the Rio Grande below Socorro and got away with 2,000 sheep. The prefect of the district, Don Ramon Luna of Valencia, decided that things had gone far enough, and he promptly raised a small army to invade the Navajo domain and chastise those responsible for the recent string of raids. At Cebolleta, Luna was joined by recruits eager to exact retribution for their own losses, and with this force he marched to Colorado Lake in western New Mexico where 500 sheep belonging to Valverde Ranch were recovered. Encouraged by this success, the expedition pushed on to the Mesa de la Vaca in eastern Arizona, at which point Luna divided his men into small units and sent

A typical Navajo hunting camp in western New Mexico. Note jerked meat drying in the background. *Courtesy Museum of New Mexico.*

them on a vengeful sweep against isolated Navajo camps. This foray netted twenty-eight prisoners, eleven oxen, 150 riding animals, and 5,000 sheep.

Well satisfied with the results of their work, members of the expedition turned back toward the Rio Grande. Ramon Luna directed his men to keep close formation on the march and watch their backtrail, since he feared the Navajos might rally and follow along in hopes of liberating the captives. At Alamitos (present-day Grants, New Mexico), thirteen Cebolletans, impatient to be with their families again, violated orders, slipped away from the main army, and started on a shortcut for their village around the western escarpment of San Mateo Peak. That night they camped in San Miguel Canyon and spent several pleasurable hours in cards around the fire before tumbling into their blankets. In the cold bleak hour before dawn, the dozing sentry slid noiselessly to the ground pincushioned with arrows, and in another instant the Navajos were upon the sleeping forms. A week later a search party from Cebolleta found the bodies and a few blood-spattered playing cards the wind had not yet claimed. Among the luckless thirteen were renowned Indian fighters Chato Aragón and Redondo Gallegos, and Pedro Chaves, brother of Manuel.[2]

In the winter of 1850-1851 pillaging by the Navajo was not confined to western New Mexico. In February Governor Calhoun wrote to the Indian commissioner in Washington outlining a list of depredations perpetrated by this tribe the length of the upper Rio Grande and to the very doors of Santa Fe. Among other outrages, he mentioned that on January 25 "near Pecos, twenty-five miles from Santa Fe, on the road to San Miguel, the Indians drove off several large flocks of sheep and other stock, killed three *pastores*, and wounded another."[3] In all likelihood, some of this theft was from flocks belonging to Lorenzo Labadie and Manuel Chaves. At least we know that by the end of February, Lorenzo had lodged a formal claim of $660 against the government for loss of livestock to Indians.[4]

Governor Calhoun's mounting anxiety over the military's inability to cope with the rising tide of Navajo incursions is reflected in his official correspondence during the months of February and March. On several occasions he described brazen attacks upon the villages surrounding Albuquerque and the turmoil that these were creating among the farming folk. About March 15 he learned that Navajo warriors had harassed the mining settlement of New Placer east of the Rio Grande and had slain one of the foremost citizens of that community, Don José María Baca. Three days later, almost in a mood of desperation, the governor issued a "Proclamation to the People of the Territory of New Mexico," in which he declared, "I recommend to all able-bodied male citizens capable of bearing arms, the formation of Volunteer Corps to protect their families, property, and homes, and as Commander-in-Chief, will commission the officers of such companies as may be raised for service against the hostile Indians."[5] Clearly, since the American military forces, spread thinly across the vast Southwestern desert, were unable to meet the Indian challenge, the governor was hoping support by a strong citizen's militia might relieve some of the pressure.

Among the first to read Governor Calhoun's proclamation and, without doubt, the first to make a direct response was Manuel Chaves. On the same day, he issued a formal set of "Proposals to Raise Six Companies of Volunteers For An Expedition to the Navajo Country." Each company was to be composed of one hundred men. Stipulations he set forth included the following: the government should furnish

100 pack mules and 600 rifles with ammunition; the volunteer forces were to be subject only to Governor Calhoun and not to any officer of the United States Army; and "The troops," in Manuel's words, "will not claim any remuneration from the government, the only recompense they ask for their services is to have the disposal of the captives, animals, cattle, &c., and they on their part promise to pursue the Navajo Nation to their extermination or complete surrender."[6]

The provision that the volunteers keep all booty seized was an old practice long used by Spain to reward militiamen who served on the frontier. The governor had specifically stated in his call that "the property which may be captured from any hostile tribe of Indians . . . shall be disposed of in accordance with the laws and customs heretofore existing in this Territory," at least until such time as Congress ruled differently.[7] Manuel's declaration to pursue the Navajo Nation to its "extermination or complete surrender" now seems a harsh one, but this was the same stern measure ultimately taken by the American military authorities in trying to resolve the Indian problem.

The death of his brother at San Miguel Canyon, added to the losses sustained by friends and relatives at Cebolleta, explain why Manuel answered with such alacrity the governor's plea for assistance. Disappointingly, no details have come to light regarding the success or failure of this Navajo campaign. It is doubtful that Manuel was able to secure the large quantity of rifles requested, since war materiel was in short supply at this juncture, but if such was the case, it probably had little effect on recruitment, since as our history has already demonstrated, the plucky New Mexicans had long been accustomed to taking on the Indians with nothing more than their own antiquated weapons.

What is important here is that a pattern was established which would prevail for the duration of the Indian wars, i.e., the civil governor appealing for citizens' aid and a few natural leaders, men such as Manuel Chaves, his friend Miguel E. Pino, and others, stepping forward to assume the burdens of command and undertaking to enroll volunteer companies. Acting in concert with regular army units of dragoons and artillery, these volunteers performed yeoman's service in safeguarding the settlements and within time earned the grudging respect of American officers, who initially had looked with some disdain upon short-term native soldiers.

The first major campaign in which Manuel Chaves earned wide acclaim was the Ute-Jicarilla War of 1855. This conflict grew out of Indian troubles along New Mexico's northern border that had steadily worsened since the year of American occupation. In 1853 famed mountain man Kit Carson, whose flair for dealing with the Indians was well-known, received a federal appointment as agent for the Ute and Jicarilla Apache tribes, the agency headquarters being established at his home in Taos.[8] Throughout that year and the next, these Indians, often acting in unison, pillaged outlying settlements and raided caravans on the Santa Fe Trail east of the mountains, feeling, of course, the growing pressure of what they considered white encroachment on their land. After soberly assessing the problem of his charges, Carson pointed out to his superiors in Washington that wild game was becoming scarce, the Indians were no longer able to support themselves by the hunt, and many were in a starving condition. As a result they indulged their natural bent for raiding in order to survive, and the situation was aggravated by an abundance of liquor they obtained from certain unscrupulous Mexicans.

"The government," he added, "can either subsist and clothe them or exterminate them."[9] Before anything else, though, the plundering had to be stopped.

Beginning in late winter of 1854, troops operating out of Fort Union, located on the edge of the plains and alongside the Santa Fe Trail, began to harry the Jicarillas, and in a series of small but important engagements over the next several months effectively reduced the ability of these Indians to wage war. But some Jicarilla die-hards fled west and took refuge with their Ute allies who roamed the mountains bordering the San Luis Valley (now southern Colorado but then a part of the Territory of New Mexico). On Christmas Day 1854, a combined war party of Utes and Jicarilla Apaches fell like a thunderbolt on the little community of Hardscrabble (now Pueblo, Colorado), killing or capturing seventeen persons and driving off all the livestock. In response to this, Brigadier General John Garland, commanding the military Department of New Mexico, laid plans for an offensive campaign to deliver a knockout blow to both tribes, just as soon as the spring thaw permitted travel over the high passes of the Sangre de Cristos. Since the general's troop strength was down to a mere 557 men for the entire territory, he realized that for any chance of success his forces would have to be bolstered by New Mexican volunteers. The new governor, David Meriwether, fully concurred with this judgment, and he issued a call, much as Calhoun had done four years before, for the enlistment of mounted volunteer companies.[10]

When this appeal was made, Manuel Chaves was at home in Santa Fe. After a hasty conference with Miguel Pino, both men decided to apply for captain's commissions over one of the six companies the governor had requested. The old warhorse Ceran St. Vrain had already been named com-

I CERTIFY, ON HONOR, That this Muster Roll exhibits the true state of Captain Manuel Chaves Company of the New Mexican Mounted Volunteers, for the period herein mentioned; that each man answers to his own proper name in person; and that the remarks set opposite the name of each officer and soldier are accurate and just.

Manuel Chaves

Commanding the Company.

Signature of Manuel Chaves on a Militia Muster Roll, Santa Fe, February 2, 1855. *Photo from the New Mexico State Records Center and Archives.*

mander with the rank of lieutenant-colonel of the new volunteer battallion, and the pair must have looked forward with pleasure to serving again under a man who enjoyed their fullest confidence. Without difficulty, Manuel was appointed captain of Company D, Mounted Volunteers, and by the end of January was actively recruiting men for his unit. Arms and supplies were to be furnished by the army, and those enrolling were expected to provide their own mounts or borrow them from their company commander.

The muster roll for Company D shows that the unit was formally organized at Santa Fe, February 2, 1855, for a term of six months. The commander, Captain Manuel Chaves, age thirty-seven, entered service with a horse valued at $150 and a packmule. Not surprisingly, the name of Román Baca, age twenty-one, appears as second-lieutenant. Both brothers, it seems, had inherited the same grand taste for adventure. Also numbered among the total complement of eighty-seven men was Manuel's servant José Armenta.[11]

The rendezvous and supply depot for all volunteer companies and regular troops was Fort Union, but the actual launching site for the expedition against the northern tribes was Taos, where most of the soldiers converged in late February. General Garland was present to oversee final preparations, although actual command of field operations was to be in the hands of Colonel Thomas T. Fauntleroy. Manuel Chaves and his men of Company D, after an uneventful journey from Santa Fe, went into camp on the edge of Taos, waiting for orders to march. Here one of the volunteers, Faustín Baca, applied for leave to go to the house of his father in San Miguel, and Manuel promptly granted it. When the general learned of this he became enraged and promptly issued orders that no furloughs be given during the campaign except in extreme cases. In his anger he called the matter to the attention of Colonel St. Vrain and was probably reminded gently that the volunteers, serving without pay, were a casual lot, and company commanders, such as Manuel Chaves, had little power to prevent their departure.[12]

During the first days of March, Colonel Fauntleroy moved his little army northward to Fort Massachusetts in the San Luis Valley adjacent to the mountain fastness where the Indians hid. Kit Carson went along in the capacity of chief guide, and in the column was a young surgeon, DeWitte C. Peters, whose writings about the operation provide us much useful information. Concerning our campaigner, one of Carson's principal biographers remarks, "This expedition of the spring of 1855 boasted no more distinguished member than Don Manuel Chaves—a worthy descendent of a DeVargas conquistador of 1690, smaller and slighter than Kit Carson, . . . and [possessing] high zest for a fight."[13] Manuel again was going to have an opportunity to show the stuff of which he was made.

The first chance came a few days after mid-March. Fauntleroy led his troops to the northern end of the San Luis Valley, and near the mouth of Saguache Pass ran upon a large camp of the enemy. A band of about 150 Jicarilla and Ute warriors skirmished with the soldiers as the women and children fled their lodges and scurried for shelter on the timbered slopes. A young Apache chief, displaying superb equestrian skill, rode in front of his warriors urging them to stand firm. As a company of volunteers bore down upon the Indian line, the chief singled out Captain Chaves in the lead and charged at him with his lance. Manuel brought his rifle up and killed the assailant with a shot, but before the Indian could fall from his horse, he was dragged to the ground and scalped by volunteer Antonio Tapia.[14] The surviving warriors were soon put to flight, and the command counted its casualties—two men wounded and two horses lost.

Surgeon Peters, who had narrowly escaped death when his runaway horse carried him among the Indians during the height of the confusion, attended to the injured and, being new to the frontier, was intrigued by the manner in which the mountain men with the column arranged "Indian style" to convey one seriously wounded soldier back to Fort Massachusetts:

> A litter is made with two long poles with shafts at each end, while the man rides in a buffalo robe tied on its sides to the poles. He has a mule before him and one behind; in other words he is in a common litter; instead of a man at each end to carry him he has two mules. You would be surprised at the places these portable beds can travel and how easy the wounded can travel in them. Lt. Col. St. Vrain who is the oldest mountaineer in this country and who is attached with the above command to the volunteers assured me he had carried a man six weeks, until his thigh united, and that he travelled himself in this way all the time he was suffering from small pox.[15]

Now that he had the Indians on the run, Colonel Fauntleroy split up his command and sent the various units to scour the mountain parks, the plains, and the Arkansas Valley beyond. St. Vrain took most of the volunteers with Dr. F.E. Kavanaugh, a surgeon and long-time resident of Taos, and went in pursuit of the Utes across the Sangre de Cristos, but Manuel's Company D remained with Fauntleroy, who now pressed north over the Wet Mountains. After advancing as far as the headwaters of Huerfano Creek, the Colonel returned to Fort Massachusetts to refit and rest his weary men. By April 20, however, he was back at his grim work; trailing north up the eastern fringe of the San Luis Valley, he sent Manuel Chaves with thirty picked men ranging ahead for Indian sign. The quest continued throughout a moonlit night, until four o'clock in the morning when Manuel rode in to report an encampment of twenty-six Indian tipis located in a side canyon off the main trail. Although the column had come ninety miles in the past thirty-two hours, the men showed themselves eager for battle, so Fauntleroy ordered them to dismount and proceed cautiously on foot. Dogs warned of their approach, but the soldiers moved into position quickly, poured a deadly fire into the camp, and within half an hour the engagement was over. Of the performance of his men, the commander testified later, "the regular troops and the officers acted with the most admirable decision and promptitude, while the conduct of the volunteers excited my warm approbation."[16]

The Colonel entrusted mopping up operations to Chaves, the results of which were reported by letter on the following day. Since this is one of the few pieces of Manuel's correspondence to survive, it is quoted here in full:

Head of San Luis Valley, New Mexico, April 30, 1855.
Col. Fauntleroy.

Sir: I have the pleasure of reporting to you that after I received your order through Lieutenant Magruder, A.A.G., to burn everything that was left by the Utes, I burned a great number of shields, bows and arrows, buck-skins and other things not worth mentioning. In the meantime, I marched up to the mountains and above the camp to the right, close to the Arkansas river, and counted forty bodies of dead Indians within three miles of the camp where we had the fight. My company found 29 horses and one mule. I do not doubt that the Indians that got away will die in a very short time, as the blood on the trail shows that they could not live long.

I remain your obedient servant,

Manuel Chaves,
Captain, N.M. Mounted Volunteers.[17]

Colonel Fauntleroy viewed his efforts thus far as highly gratifying. The Jicarilla and the Ute had been given no rest throughout the spring and had been made to feel the sting of American military power. Moving down to Taos, he called in the several wings of his command, intending to regroup and take the field still again, but the enlistment term of the volunteer units was swiftly drawing to an end, and as a result plans were abandoned for any large scale action. Colonel St. Vrain, nevertheless, was intent upon putting the last few weeks of his battallion's enlistment to good use, so taking the best of his volunteer companies, he made one final sweep through the hostile country as far as the Huerfano. Going north the now battle-hardened veterans under Manuel Chaves were detailed to scout the valley of Vermejo Creek, but nothing was found. After the company rejoined St. Vrain's main force in Colorado, a large party of Indians was observed approaching through a stand of pines, and the Colonel carefully laid an ambush. But the surprise was spoiled when one of Manuel's men accidentally discharged his gun, causing the Indians to fade quickly into the forest.[18]

By the end of July, St. Vrain had his soldiers back in Taos with little to show for their last long ride north. Within a week, the companies had all been mustered out of service, and the volunteer battallion was officially dissolved. But its aid in support of the regular army troops had been crucial and had insured the overall success of the campaign. Ute and Jicarilla resistance was permanently broken and during the summer their chiefs visited the Indian Agency in Taos to sue for peace. The men who had followed St. Vrain—Chaves and other captains—could return home assured that their efforts had helped bring some measure of tranquility to the troubled frontier.

Scarcely had the fires of war subsided along the northern border, however, when a new blaze flared up in the south, where fierce bands of Mogollon, Gila, and Coyotero Apaches unleashed murderous raids against towns and ranches. By 1857 the situation had become critical, a fact painfully evident when in the summer of that year, Indian Agent H.L. Dodge was murdered by Coyoteros near Zuñi. Colonel B.L.E. Bonneville, in temporary command of military affairs during the absence of General Garland, determined to bring the raiders under control and at the same time enhance an already modest reputation he enjoyed as a scourge of the Indians. To do this he formed the Gila Expedition, composed of southern and northern columns with himself directing operations of the first and Colonel William Wing Loring, commandant of Fort Union, the second. The strategy was to be the same employed successfully against the Ute and Jicarilla—assail the Indians in their own country, give them no rest, and compel them to seek peace on the white man's terms. But as it developed, "Bonneville's War" was to be a limited affair, lasting only several weeks in June.

Early in the month, Colonel Loring and his command of approximately three hundred struck off in a southwesterly direction from the Rio Grande toward the mountain wilderness surrounding the headwaters of the Gila River. His scouts and guides were members of Captain Chaves' "Spy Company."[19] Presumably Manuel's performance during the Colorado campaign had strongly impressed his superiors, and when this new mission arose, he was asked to serve as chief of scouts. Under terms of his enlistment, he was to draw three dollars per day and one ration, and he received a free hand in selecting the men to be the eyes and ears of the column. Román Baca, of course, was first at his side, and Lorenzo Labadie joined his hardriding kinsmen, as did Don Jesus Chaves, whose exact relationship to Manuel, though said to be close, is not known.[20]

Loring's trail wound through a rough, mountainous country seamed with deep canyons. This was the heart of Apacheria, as yet unknown to the Americans and scarcely more familiar to the New Mexicans. When sign was discovered of the passing of a large party of Indians, the colonel called a council of his officers and scouts to discuss the best way to proceed. After all others had spoken, Loring turned to Chaves, silent until now, and asked for his judgment.

"Colonel," he replied in slow and measured words, "I am a soldier and came here to obey orders, but now that I am asked my opinion I'll say there's only one way to go about this. We must follow the trail day and night, making no fires, and eating cold rations. We'll have to move rapidly, because once they know we're on their trail, they'll skip for the border and be in Mexico before we get in sight of them. But if you will allow me to go ahead with my company, I know I can overtake them."[21]

Loring recognized the soundness in this advice, and though realizing it would put his men to a severe strain, he gave his assent. Manuel and his companions were seen infrequently in the days that followed, as they ranged ahead picking up sign and setting an exhausting pace. The scouts, indeed, appeared indestructible, bred as they were to the hardships of this savage land, but not so the troopers, who soon succumbed to fatigue and commenced falling asleep in their saddles. Loring finally called a halt and ordered a night's rest, knowing his trail-weary soldiers would be useless even if they managed to come up with the enemy. Sometime after midnight, Manuel rode in to report. The grueling march had not been bootless. The Indians with a flock of stolen sheep were encamped in a steep-walled canyon a short distance beyond, the large number of fires indicating that it was a sizable party.

The colonel let his men rest awhile longer, then had them out of their blankets, much refreshed, and moving noiselessly toward the canyon. Near the rim in the predawn darkness, he paused to plan the attack. Several of the junior officers argued for splitting the command, sending one part below and the other above the Indian camp, and snaring the enemy in a squeeze. But Manuel strongly objected. Time did not allow for such cautious maneuvering, and the only course giving hope for success was to dismount, dash on foot down the precipitous slope, and be in the camp before the Indians could rally. One of the young officers, perhaps miffed at being overruled by a volunteer, declared this was a barbarous proposition—far too dangerous, he said, to unhorse the troopers and send them amongst foes whose numbers were uncertain, to fight, every man for himself. With some perturbation, Manuel rested his case: "Well this is how we New Mexicans fight, and for those who have the stomach for it, it is the best way."[22]

Colonel Loring effected something of a compromise. Cutting out the complaining officer with a small detachment, he sent him along the rim as a support unit and then turning to Manuel, he announced, "Now Captain, I will go down the precipice with you."[23] And below they went like a wave, the crest of their charge rolling over the encampment, engulfing the dismayed Apaches. Eight of the enemy were slain, including the notorious chief Cuchillo Negro (Black Knife), while survivors fled up the narrow valley, abandoning their camp possessions and livestock. Pursuit brought the soldiers to a neighboring canyon where they discovered another band of Indians, but these escaped leaving behind 500 sheep.[24]

The exultant soldiers regrouped and gathered in the spoils: a flock of 1,500 sheep, skin tents and field equipage, a large quantity of packed meat, and ten captives. Loring roamed the area for another few days looking for strays, but water and grass were short and he must have viewed with some relief an order which reached him calling an end to the campaign. Bonneville had met some small success in prosecuting his war against the Apaches further south in the region of the Burro and Florida Mountains, but General Garland, who had returned to New Mexico and resumed command during the summer, concluded that, while the expedition appeared useful, it had been initiated without proper authority.[25]

Many citizens who had suffered from the ravages of Cuchillo Negro's band were elated over the success of the operation, and a Santa Fe paper referred to the Gila Expedition as "the most arduous, trying, and dangerous since New Mexico became a possession of the United States government."[26] Colonel Loring, who had showed himself a model commander, gave full credit to his officers and men for "enduring with unflinching fortitude" the rigors of a difficult march.[27] But he reserved his most glowing praise

Colonel William W. Loring, Manuel Chaves' commander during the Gila Expedition of 1857. Loring lost his left arm in the Mexican War, served the South in the Civil War, and after the defeat of the Confederacy joined the army of the Khedive of Egypt.

for his chief of scouts, whose aptitude for trailing, judicious counsel, and unassailable coolness in battle had been most responsible for victory and the laurels it brought to the entire troop.

It is worth noting here that with the outbreak of the Civil War, Loring resigned his commission and entered the service of the Confederacy, rising to the rank of major-general. Then with defeat, he followed many of his fellow officers into exile, serving conspicuously for ten years in the army of the Khedive of Egypt. In later years, enfeebled by wounds, he returned to this country and took up residence at the Union League Club in Philadelphia, where he spent the rest of his days composing his memoirs. In them he paid tribute to his old comrade Manuel Chaves, who had served him so gallantly on the far New Mexico frontier. Had Manuel lived in the Middle Ages, he declared with feeling, doubtless he would have been a second El Cid, the great chivalric hero of Spain.[28] Coming from a man of Loring's stature, this was no trivial compliment.

Another incident requiring his skill at tracking Indians overtook Manuel Chaves soon after his release from the Gila campaign. That we know so much concerning this particular episode is owed entirely to a book entitled *The Marvelous Country,* written by one of the first Southwestern tourists, Samuel Woodworth Cozzens. With several dauntless companions, Cozzens roved over much of southern New Mexico and Arizona during the late 1850s and early 1860s, precisely the years when Apache incursions were at their peak. It was probably in 1858 when the Cozzens party was outfitting at La Mesilla, located on the Rio Grande above El Paso, that the tragedy of the White family occurred.

Doubtless as a result of political influence, a young Philadelphian, E.J. White, had received appointment as post sutler for Fort Buchanan, which lay near the Sonoita River southwest of Tucson. Traveling from the East by ship, White with his wife and infant arrived at Port Lavaca, Texas, procured a mule-drawn ambulance and two Mexican servants, and in the company of a wagon caravan started west over the Butterfield Trail. Finding the pace of the train overly tedious and eager to reach its new home, the family pushed ahead to the New Mexican village of La Mesilla which was reached late on a summer's evening. Because accommodations were scarce, Samuel Cozzens came forward with an offer to share his house, since, as he explained, "His party was quite delighted with the good fortune that had once more brought us in contact with an American lady; for American ladies in that country are like angels' visits, few and far between."

"I found Mrs. White a charming little woman," he continued, "about twenty-five years of age, refined and highly educated. She informed me that this was the first time she had ever left her father's roof; yet now with her babe she had left her luxurious home in the old Quaker City, and for nearly two months had been 'roughing it' on the road from Texas."

Out of hearing of Mrs. White, Cozzens impressed upon her husband the need for vigilance as the country beyond was known to be infested with Apaches. The next day he accompanied the travelers several hours on their journey, leaving them about three o'clock in the afternoon with further words of caution. On the following morning, Cozzens was aroused from his bed by the beating of a drum and a great commotion in the plaza. Hastily drawing on his clothes, he hurried out to find an excited throng of Mexicans listening to the tale of two ranchers who had just come in from the Rio Membres. About midnight the pair had encountered the bodies of two men, one American and one Mexican, both scalped, and a little further on the remains of an ambulance still smoking. A few articles they had retrieved from broken trunks left no doubt that the victims of the disaster were the young White couple. But the ranchers found no bodies of a woman or child, which indicated they had been carried into captivity.

Heartsick over the news, Cozzens mounted his horse and rode with urgency to nearby Fort Fillmore, where he received assurance that a squad of dragoons would be dispatched in pursuit as soon as possible. On returning to La Mesilla, he discovered that about fifty Mexicans had assembled in the plaza with their horses and rifles, determined to start after the Indians at once. Cozzens and a half dozen other Americans present immediately volunteered to join the rescue company, and, as he tells us, the men were greatly encouraged because as scouts they had "two of the most celebrated guides in the country, Don Manuel Chaves and Don Jesus Armijo." What circumstances may have brought Manuel to La Mesilla at this critical moment are not known. Since the town was astride the main road south, perhaps he was on a journey to Mexico. Or possibly he had just been released from another military expedition of which we have no knowledge. In any event, the need for his services had never been more desperate.

A ride of two hours brought the party to the macabre scene of the massacre. The bodies of White and a servant were discovered by the roadside riddled with arrows, mangled, and half devoured by wolves. Around them could be seen traces of a terrible struggle, evidence that the men had fought savagely but futilely to beat off the attack. Manuel and his fellow scout, Jesus Armijo, went over the ground meticulously and concluded that a band of fifteen Apaches had carried off Mrs. White and her child and had fled south toward the Florida Mountains.

"Swiftly and silently we sped on our errand of mercy," says Cozzens. Mindful of the need for haste, the men passed at full gallop over a hard, pebbly plain, pausing only occasionally to allow Manuel to dismount and examine the trail. At dusk they rode into an oasis of a valley containing a clear meandering stream. After a brief rest the frantic pace was resumed under the light of a full moon. Near dawn the tired horsemen came to a spring which issued from beneath a hugh boulder. Fresh tracks at the water's edge showed that they were fast closing the gap, so the leaders called a halt, intending to wait for the soldiers to catch up before encountering the Indians. A few moments later, however, one of the men let out a yell. He had discovered the tiny body of Mrs. White's child lying under a bush and lanced through and through by Apache spears. The entire company was sickened by the grisly spectacle, and on all sides broke muttered curses in Spanish. To delay revenge was now unthinkable, and after the briefest rest for the horses, the pursuit was resumed. Two hours hard riding down a canyon brought the party again upon an open plain. The scouts pointed south toward the far horizon and all eyes discerned a thin plume of blue smoke ascending from the foothills of the Floridas. The Apaches had gone into camp.

The pursuers now swung wide to take advantage of shelter afforded by a spur of the mountains, and, undetected, they approached within a few miles of their game. Conferring with the scouts, Samuel Cozzens urged an immediate attack, but Manuel Chaves, who knew the nature of his foe only too well, forbade it. At the first sign of trouble, he warned, the Indians would kill their captive. The only chance was to slip up on the camp and cut down the Apaches swiftly before they could recover from surprise. After admonishing the others to remain quiet, Manuel took Jesus Armijo and set out to reconnoiter the terrain.

"Nothing could be done but wait for their return," relates Cozzens. "We threw ourselves upon the ground and gazed into the bright blue dome over our heads . . . while we listened to marvellous tales told by some of the men of the skill and cunning of the guides who had gone to the enemy camp."

The hours dragged slowly by until late afternoon when a new smoke was observed, indicating the Indians intended to remain encamped for the night. At dark the scouts returned and reported they had seen Mrs. White, who, worn out from fatigue from her horrible journey, was apparently sleeping. The situation would be dangerous, but by waiting for the Indians to sleep, the rescue had some chance of success.

At the appropriate hour, Manuel divided the company. Taking half the men, he stole below the Apaches, leaving the remainder with Jesus Armijo to find positions on the hillside above the camp. At a prearranged signal, the cry of a whippoorwill, the riflemen were to fire and rush instantly upon the Indians. From a berth among the rocks and an arm's length from Jesus Armijo, Samuel Cozzens peered down into a moonlit bowl. Two blanket-wrapped figures crouched over the embers of a fire, while other shadowy forms could be seen stretched on the ground nearby. Cozzens searched in vain for some sign of Mrs. White, then Armijo touched his shoulder and pointed to a small copse of stunted pines. At that moment an Apache rose from the fire and walked among the trees.

As Cozzens recalled later, "Waiting for the signal from Don Manuel seemed an eternity. At last from the hill upon the opposite side of the damp, we hear the low mournful notes of a whip-poor-will, so natural and so truthful that it seems to us it must be the cry of the bird itself." Don Jesus answered with a similar call, and suddenly twenty rifles cracked as one. Most of the sleeping figures twitched and lay still, but several leaped from their robes and broke for the woods. Pell-mell the men rushed from the hillside, down through the camp, and into the thicket of pines. There they came upon Mrs. White, seemingly asleep on the ground, but as a torch was brought up, they perceived blood gushing from a dozen stab wounds. "Her still warm body," lamented Cozzens, "bore testimony to the sad fact that the sound of our rifles had proved her death-knell."

All the men were stricken, and none more than Manuel Chaves. Their best efforts had not been enough to deliver the unfortunate woman, and nothing was left now but to consign her remains to a lonely grave beneath the shadow of the Florida Mountains. "And there she reposes," Cozzens ended his tale, "the elegant, accomplished, and refined lady, her grave unmarked and unknown."[29] In claiming victims, this brutal frontier made no distinction between the innocent and the malevolent.

Springs in this narrow arroyo furnished water and suggested the name for Manuel Chaves' Hacienda de Ojuelos. *Author photo.*

8

Hacienda de Ojuelos

Sometime toward the end of the 1850s, Manuel Chaves moved his family to the ranch at Ojuelos, located near the eastern edge of the old Tomé Land Grant. The history of this property is obscure, but in all probability it was established originally as a sheep camp by Manuel's father-in-law, Don Pablo Labadie. Both Manuel and Lorenzo Labadie had continued to struggle with livestock operations in the Pecos Valley, but their success there had been meager, since other business commitments forced them to leave the management in the hands of *mayordomos* or foremen. Since about 1855, Lorenzo had occupied various posts in the Indian Superintendency of New Mexico, and, as we have seen, on at least one occasion he served under his brother-in-law in the campaign against Cuchillo Negro's Apaches.

Ojuelos (meaning "springs") was an ideal site for a stock-raising venture. Situated on an elevated flat on the western slope of the Manzano Mountains, the ranch overlooked league upon league of prime grassland that fell in a sweeping curve down to the green belt of the *bosque* marking the course of the Rio Grande. Near the river could be seen the dark, rounded hump of the Cerro de Tomé that served the nearby villagers as a lookout; beyond, across the river and the valley, bristled the serrated, angular ridge of Ladrón or Thieves Mountain. Ojuelos offered not only abundant grass and an awe-inspiring view, but, as its name implied, a plentiful supply of water. An upper spring (referred to as Lo de Arriba) poured into a small natural bowl on the side of a sandy hill, while a lower one (Lo de Abajo) issued from beneath cottonwoods in a narrow arroyo a hundred yards to the north.

The springs had long attracted Indian travelers and in prehistoric times even a few permanent residents, who built small clusters of adobe and rock dwellings to form a diminutive farming settlement.[1] Foot trails led east out of Ojuelos up deep canyons that slashed through the Manzanos, and then climbed over the crest and descended to the buffalo plains beyond. After the Spaniards came, a wagon road from Albuquerque followed the high ground at the foot of the mountains and passed by the springs on its way to Abó Pass twenty miles to the south. That this choice site remained unsettled during the colonial period may be attributed to its exposed and isolated position which discouraged even the most iron-hearted of Spaniards. As far as we know, Manuel Chaves was the first white man to make a serious attempt to develop and hold these springs and the surrounding plains.[2]

How much his in-laws had already built at their sheep camp cannot be determined; probably no more than crude *jacal* structures for the shepherds. But Manuel needed a substantial and comfortable house for his family, and one, heavily fortified, that could withstand the severest Indian attack. So on a level bench below the two springs, he put his servants and peon laborers to building with native stone a dwelling that would satisfy his requirements. Loopholes pierced the stout walls on all sides, although a totally foreboding aspect was avoided by placing a spacious *portal*, or porch, along the front, from the shaded coolness of which the family could survey the unbroken vista to the west. In the foothills above the house lay deposits of varied-colored soils: white, grey, mauve, sienna, and yellow—all useful for soft, pastel-hued plaster in rooms of a hacienda. There, too, were banks of red clay where the Indian women of the kitchen could find material for *ollas*, bowls, and cups. Under Manuel's direction, some of the men, working with wooden shovels and scoops, dug a small *acequia* to funnel water from the springs down to a dirt tank alongside the house, where a grove of cottonwoods soon sprouted. Other ditches led to tiny truck gardens, tightly fenced with adobe walls to keep out horses, burros, and deer. Some attempts at dry farming were initiated below the house, and within a short time, Manuel was sending out his shepherds and flocks to the far corners of his domain. Like most of its counterparts in New Mexico, the Chaves hacienda at Ojuelos was virtually self-sufficient, producing all but a few iron goods and foodstuffs needed by the household.

From the front *portal* of their home, Manuel and Vicenta could look seventeen miles westward and in the rarefied New Mexican air easily distinguish the spire of the church jutting above the trees in the old Tomé plaza. With that landmark to nudge his memory, we may be sure that Don Manuel found occasion to tell his children of the Tomé massacre that had brought such sorrow to their ancestors almost a century before. In the belfry of the church, two

Ruins of the Manuel Chaves hacienda at Ojuelos about 1918. *Photo from Amado Chaves collection.*

Ruins of the Manuel Chaves hacienda at Ojuelos about 1918. *Photo from Amado Chaves collection.*

Boleslo Romero of Tomé who played among the ruins of the Ojuelos ranch during his youth stands on the site of the hacienda, today marked only by low mounds. *Author photo.*

The author, right, and Boleslo Romero of Tomé examine the remains of one of the giant cottonwoods that once shaded the Manuel Chaves hacienda at Ojuelos. *George Pearl photo.*

bells of different tone spoke a language all their own, the ringing notes carrying messages and news clearly to distant Ojuelos and all parts of the grant. At *doblar las campanas*, or tolling of the bells, outlying ranches sent in their riders to learn who had died and the date of the funeral. A different cadence warned of approaching Indians and summoned the militia, while still another proclaimed a fiesta. These bells still ring today in Tomé, but their notes are dimmed by the unconscious noise level of our motorized civilization, and they can no longer be heard at Ojuelos.

José Antonio Márquez, who died only a few years ago in Tomé, as a youth worked for Don Manuel. On one memorable morning, he and another boy were sent to Comanche Canyon southeast of Ojuelos to collect firewood in an oxcart. While the two were resting at noon, several Apaches crept up on them, using juniper branches as a screen. José saw them first, shouted a warning, and leaped over the ox that had lain down in the shade. One of the Indians, rushing in pursuit, was tumbled in the dust as the frightened animal lunged to its feet, but another, springing on his horse, came pounding after José. Each time he leaned down to snatch up his prey, the boy dropped flat on the ground, and the horse carried the warrior on past. In a breathless heat José finally reached Ojuelos, and as the Apache fled, he threw himself over an adobe wall where several peons were working. A rescue party quickly formed and raced back to the canyon. But José's companion had vanished, carried into captivity.[3]

On occasion the Indians were so bold as to ride up to the very doors of the Ojuelos hacienda. Once the children were playing under the cottonwoods, when young Amado let out a scream and ran toward the house. Manuel appeared on the *portal* with rifle in hand and beheld a mounted

Apache thundering through the yard with little Irineo tucked under his arm. Knowing he was taking a chance that his son might be injured or killed, he drew a steady bead and shot the Indian cleanly. Irineo dropped head first on the hard sod and was knocked unconscious, but he was spared a captive's fate that was the lot of so many other New Mexican lads.[4]

If all the encounters Manuel Chaves had with the Indians on his Ojuelos ranch were known, their recital might well form a lengthy narrative. But two especially stand out, since the details were passed by word of mouth throughout northern New Mexico and helped mold the legend of the Little Lion. In the spring of 1860, Manuel, accompanied by his son Amado, went to one of the lambing camps at a place called Salada. While there, an excited messenger arrived from Manuel's cousin J. Francisco Chaves (son of the late Mariano), warning that a raiding party of Apaches was heading in that direction. Assembling the shepherds, who were shaking with fear at news of Indians, Manuel inspected their muskets and assigned places to each among the rocks and trees. But no alarm was raised that day and the men slept on their arms. The following morning one of the shepherds hurried into camp from his flock with word of a dust cloud to the west. Manuel rode up on a small knoll and with his field glass counted twenty-two Indians carrying seventeen rifles.

Back in camp he called his men together and held them close around their breakfast fire. Nobody was to move, he ordered, until the enemy drew near, then they could scatter to their posts and await his signal to fire. If all went well, perhaps they might throw a good scare into these Apaches. From Ojuelos, Manuel had brought out a box of cakes and other sweets prepared by Vicenta, and this he calmly opened, distributing the contents to the nervous, fidgety shepherds.

Not until the Indians were within 500 yards did Manuel allow his men to seek shelter. Then taking Amado by the hand, he ran up the hill to his own tree. The Apaches, seeing the frantic running, concluded they had put the New Mexicans to flight, and imprudently they rushed into the camp. Two warriors spied beside the fire Chaves' silver mounted saddle and bridle and a valuable Navajo blanket. One of them leaned from his horse to scoop up the blanket, but suddenly went sprawling with a bullet in his head from Manuel's rifle. The prize fell into a kettle of *atole,* or blue corn meal, the shepherds had been preparing for breakfast, and the second Indian swung down to retrieve it. But Manuel had rammed home another ball, and he caught the blanket thief with a shot in the neck.

The firing now became general as the Apaches realized they had blundered into a hornet's nest. Between shots Manuel looked down the slope to a small juniper where he had tied his two fine horses. One of his best men Concepción Baca had been placed on guard there, but to his disgust, he saw several Indians ride up and take the animals unchallenged. When the battle sputtered out with the Apaches in retreat, he strode angrily down the hill and confronted Baca. But his man had a strange story. Concepción had been taken from his Sonora home in boyhood by the Apaches and had been raised by them until recaptured in New Mexico and adopted by a prominent member of the Baca family, a fact well known to Manuel. As the Indians had approached the horses and Concepción raised his rifle, he had recognized the leader as the same old Apache who had raised him and had inflicted so many beatings and torments. All the inbred boyhood terror swept over him again in an instant, and he froze, unable to pull the trigger.[5] Manuel understood, and he called in his shepherds, who had gone among the fallen Apaches taking scalps.

Not long after the fight at Salada, Don Juan Cristobál Armijo, a close friend of Manuel, sent his son to Ojuelos with the message that Apaches had stolen 200 mules along the Rio Grande and were in precipitous flight toward the Manzano Mountains. He and a party were in pursuit, but fearing they would not overtake the raiders before they reached the high country, he asked Manuel to gather some men and head them off. El Leoncito was alone at his ranch, but he had never yet failed to heed a plea for help.

"How many Apaches," he asked young Armijo.

"Twenty or so," replied the boy.

"Well, come then lad. You and me, we'll stop them."

"Not much. I'm no fool, Don Manuel."

And so, alone, Chaves bridled his fleetest mare, and swinging his ponderous muzzle-loader across the pommel of his saddle, he galloped out of Ojuelos to intercept the Indians. South of the ranch, he ascended a timbered ridge, from which point he could see the thieves riding toward him and driving the mules. Several miles behind, a dust cloud showed the position of the pursuers.

Incredibly the little man of leonine spirit rode out of the timber directly in the path of the Apaches. As he did, he swung his arm in a wide circle as if signaling to men in the trees, and the bluff worked. The Indians, never imagining that anyone would face them without a large force at his back, let out a yell and scattered like quail, abandoning their plundered stock. Manuel waited until Don Cristobál and his men came up to recover the mules, and then he started for the ranch. En route, his mare stepped in a hole and fell on him, breaking his leg. In severe pain, he remounted and continued the journey, taking this mishap in his stride as he did all else. For him, this bit of ill-luck would mean three months in bed and a slight limp the rest of his life.[6]

Although Manuel Chaves had his hands full protecting his family and caring for his sheep business at Ojuelos, he still found time, during the years just prior to the Civil War, to lead volunteer companies against his old enemies, the Navajos. A treaty with these Indians, concluded on Christmas Day 1858, had established a line running north and south through Bear Springs as the tribe's eastern boundary, but since the Navajos were accustomed to roam at will, they gave it scant attention. The following summer a band of renegades murdered several persons and seized cattle within ten miles of Santa Fe, an incident that threw citizens of the capital into an uproar. In an indignant frame of mind, members of the territorial legislature passed a law authorizing private citizens to organize their own volunteer militia companies to chastise the marauders.

Colonel Thomas Fauntleroy, who had become departmental commander in October of 1859, was strictly opposed to the volunteers invading the Navajo country without supervision, for he felt this would only lead to further reprisals by the Indians and prolong hostilities. Fauntleroy was a rarity among frontier military officers. He believed the Navajos should be treated fairly but firmly and that invasion of their homeland should be made only in pursuit of specific offenders, leaving innocent persons undisturbed. Unfortunately the times were not propitious for his policy of moderation. A series of raids along the Rio Grande, combined with the attack near Santa Fe, outraged farmers and ranchers, who now brought pressure upon Governor Abraham Rencher. Fearing the army was incapable of providing protection, the governor approved the legislature's call for the formation of militia companies, noting that "our people prefer to carry on Indian wars in their own way," and "citizens have the duty and necessity of providing means to protect themselves."[7] Over this issue Rencher and Fauntleroy clashed openly, with the latter refusing to supply militiamen ammunition as had been customary in the past.[8]

Those who had suffered at the hands of the Navajos formed a convention that met in Santa Fe during August of 1860. Some money was subscribed, a call for a regiment of mounted volunteers was made, and officers were appointed. Miguel Pino, a leader in this movement, won election as colonel of the regiment, and, probably following his suggestion, a message was sent to Manuel Chaves at Ojuelos, requesting him to serve as lieutenant-colonel. During ensuing weeks, preparations continued and on September 17 militiamen were formally enrolled at various towns in northern New Mexico. Manuel's cousin, J. Francisco Chaves, raised a company of 134 men and four officers at the village of Peralta, while other units were formed at Santa Cruz de la Cañada, San Miguel, Bernalillo, and Santa Fe. The total troop strength came to almost 450, the men furnishing their own arms, horses, rations, and clothing. A large number of pack animals, however, was requisitioned from private citizens for use by the campaigners.

By September 23 all companies had converged at the small settlement of San Isidro near the Navajo frontier, where they underwent review by New Mexico's Adjutant-General M.L. Cotton.[9] The available documents indicate that Manuel Chaves was actually in charge of the expedition, with Colonel Pino remaining in Santa Fe. By this time it almost goes without saying that when Manuel took the field, his loyal brother Román was at his right hand, on this occasion serving as a scout.

The regiment followed the old Jemez Trail south to Laguna Pueblo, then veered west to Bear Springs, a site which Manuel remembered well from his boyhood experience with the Navajo. Although details are sketchy, it seems the command was divided, its separate detachments being sent to scour the Tunicha Mountains and the country as far as the Hopi Pueblos in eastern Arizona. This was vast, arid country, the heart of Navajoland and difficult to cross on horseback. The severity of the march is confirmed by the fact that several of the companies lost over 50 percent of their mounts, "from fatigue and want of forage," according to the official report, while one unit saw thirty-three of its forty mules perish.

Such assiduous harrying of the Navajos, however, produced results, and a number of small skirmishes were fought. In one of these, Román Baca distinguished himself in a manner that was not soon forgotten by his comrades. He had come along as a scout and common volunteer, as much to serve under his now famous brother as to satisfy his craving for adventure. Ambitious to be a captain, nevertheless, he did not wish it said that he was promoted because of his relationship to the commander. So at the opening of a fierce fight, he said to Colonel Chaves, "Tell me something to do to earn a captaincy."

At that moment a Navajo was riding at the head of his companions, waving a red blanket and defying the New Mexicans. "Do you see that Indian?" Manuel said, pointing. "Bring him down and I'll make you a captain."

Román let out a war whoop, leaped on his horse, and sped out in the open. The Navajo recognized the challenge and spurred up to the charge. He fired first, but missed, and never got a second chance. Román shot him in the chest, slid off his horse and scalped him, then raced back to his lines under a rain of bullets and arrows. He was given his captaincy on the spot.[10]

As far as the militiamen were concerned, the results of the expedition were satisfying. The Navajo had been given a sound drubbing in their own yard, a large number of livestock were recovered, and some captives, mostly women and children, were taken. Probably the campaign would have continued longer, but both ammunition and horses gave out, so in early December Manuel ordered a return to the settlements. Navajo hostilities were by no means ended with this foray, but it had been shown that the New Mexicans, acting under their own competent leader and campaigning in a country they knew intimately, could perform as well or better than regular army troops.

Later the same winter, acting upon orders of the secretary of war, Colonel Fauntleroy sent out his own expedition in an effort to curb Navajo hostilities. He did so, however, with extreme reluctance. His position on the matter was stated in these words:

> The unfortunate relations which have rendered these operations necessary, and which will probably occasion much suffering to all concerned in them, may be justly attributed in part to a system of retaliatory and predatory incursions, which have been carried on by the people of this Territory against the Navajos for some time past, and which has been sanctioned by the territorial governor.[11]

This view, although quite accurate, must be measured against the claim of the Indian agent for New Mexico, who reported that during the years 1859 and 1860, three hundred persons had been killed by the Indians, fifty-five of these being miners slain by Navajos along the San Juan and Animas rivers.[12]

Since Fauntleroy was hard pressed by public clamor, civil officials, and his military superiors to end these Indian depredations, he found himself obliged to subordinate his own views to the demands of his office. Thus he assigned Brevet Lieutenant-Colonel Edward R.S. Canby to undertake a six-week campaign against the Navajos and to enlist in support Manuel Chaves, Román Baca, and a troop of New Mexican volunteers.

Canby entered the field, engaged the Indians in several minor tilts, appropriated some of their sheep, and attempted to negotiate with their band leaders. Although he failed to accomplish any permanent reform in the Navajo's conduct, he did persuade a number of the less bellicose chiefs to submit to a twelve-month armistice. The problem was that numerous young renegades, called *ladrones* (thieves), refused to acknowledge authority of the chiefs and posed a serious threat to maintenance of the truce.

The story of one curious incident during Canby's expedition has been preserved. The colonel was encamped somewhere in western New Mexico when Román Baca, who with twenty New Mexicans had been scouting near Cienaga Amarilla, rode in with a captured Navajo. Hearing of the prisoner, Canby ordered him brought to his tent. But he had not reckoned with the independence of the volunteers.

"Tell Colonel Canby for me," said young Baca curtly, "that if he wants a Navajo, he had better go and catch one as I did." And he promptly hanged the Indian to a tree in front of the camp.

Just as promptly, Canby dispatched a lieutenant with an armed escort to arrest the insubordinate scout, but Román took up his rifle and threatend to shoot it out if the order was obeyed.

"He means what he says," warned Manuel Chaves, who was standing nearby, observing but not participating in the altercation. The officer went back to report, and the colonel felt constrained to let the matter drop. The volunteers plainly supported Román to a man, and deep in hostile country Canby could ill afford a division in his ranks.[13]

The series of Navajo incidents in 1860 and early 1861 provide a backdrop for one of the strangest episodes in the life of Manuel Chaves. On August 8, 1861, he took command of Fort Fauntleroy, which was then garrisoned by a regiment of New Mexican Mounted Volunteers.[14] The post, named for the commanding officer of the department, had been established on August 31, 1860, at Bear Springs, principally to serve as a deterrent to Indian war parties.[15] There was some irony, perhaps, in the fact that Manuel was returning to assume command of a military post located on the very site, where, as a boy, he had bathed his multiple wounds administered by the Navajos. As commander, his principal duty was to bend all efforts toward preserving the shaky armistice established by Canby earlier in the year. This meant he was to employ his men in patrolling the frontier to prevent unauthorized expeditions and unlicensed traders from stirring up the Indians. By a directive issued September 2 from military headquarters in Santa Fe, Manuel was advised that the armistice might be extended for another six months, provided the Navajos cooperated. Therefore, he was to take advantage of every opportunity to impress the chiefs with the fact that final arrangement of a permanent peace treaty hinged upon their continuing good behavior.[16]

Not knowing how long his services might be required

Fort Wingate, successor of Fort Fauntleroy, at Bear Springs, in the late nineteenth century.
Ben Wittick photo, courtesy Museum of New Mexico.

at Fort Fauntleroy, it is logical to surmise that Manuel had removed his wife and children from Ojuelos and for safety placed them with relatives, perhaps at Peralta or Albuquerque. It is known that on at least one occasion, he brought them from the Rio Grande in a family carriage for a brief visit at the fort. On returning, the vehicle became mired in the mud crossing Blue Water Creek, and Manuel climbed down to help the driver. While pulling on a rope, he lost one of his most treasured possessions, a gold ring engraved with the Chaves coat-of-arms. Though all the party joined in a search, the heirloom was never recovered.[17]

Manuel had been in charge of Fort Fauntleroy less than a month when an affair arose that seriously jeopardized his career and almost led to a renewed outbreak of Navajo hostilities. The incident involved a disputed horse race between soldiers at the post and visiting Indians, and since at least four different versions of the tumultuous event are recorded, getting at the truth is a difficult matter. And none of the stories comes from the Navajo, their side remaining untold.[18] However, by sifting the several accounts and piecing together the most plausible bits of information, the picture emerges something like this.

For several weeks in late summer of 1861, Dr. F.E. Kavenaugh, who did double duty as regimental surgeon and post sutler, had been racing a fine thoroughbred Kentucky horse with spectacular success.[19] None of the soldiers with their scrubby mounts could hope to compete with him, but the Navajos, who came to the fort in large numbers each day to draw rations of meat and flour, were eager to try their luck. The Indians, in fact, were so strongly addicted to racing that it formed almost an obsession. They gambled away money, goods, horses, and wives and would return as soon as new stakes could be gathered. After a few bouts with Dr. Kavenaugh's thoroughbred, it began to appear that they were permanently disadvantaged.

Apparently the New Mexican militiamen, especially the officers, were gamblers in their own right. Since they had little with which to wager, they sometimes resorted to betting government horses. If they won, they sold their take in animals to the post supply master for remounts, and if they lost, which only happened when the thoroughbred was not running, friendly clerks could usually be counted upon to juggle the books and cover up the shortage.

One day in early September, a group of soldiers was in the sutler's store, which served as a sort of social forum and club, when a half-dozen Navajos under Chief Miguelito appeared. The Indians were warmly received, and Miguelito asked to speak with the commanding officer, Colonel Chaves. When told that Chaves was ill at the fort, he singled out Captain José D. Sena and told him that his people had a prize horse with which they wished to challenge Dr. Kavenaugh's thoroughbred. The terms of the race were quickly agreed upon, the date was set for a week hence, and the Indians departed in good spirits.

In the days that followed, the soldiers' horse became the subject of great attention, as he was pampered and exercised to bring him to peak condition. Lieutenant Rafael Ortiz, light of weight and an accomplished horseman, was selected as rider. Rumors floated in concerning the excitement among the Navajos and of strange ceremonies being conducted to insure an Indian victory. According to the stories, native priests worked spells over small wooden images of horses, reciting prayers and incantations. Perhaps word of these rites was deliberately leaked to the troops in an effort to unnerve them. But if so, no such effect was achieved.

Race day arrived—one of those crystalline September days for which New Mexico is still famous. The Navajos streamed in from their camps, bearing great quantities of blankets and buckskins and driving herds of horses and mules to bet against the soldiers. All wagered animals were placed in a corral near the parade ground under the watchful eye of the Officer of the Day; when one horse was bet against another, the pair was tied together and turned into the enclosure. If cash was put up against a piece of buckskin, the money was bound in a corner of the skin, together with names of the two parties.

Two lesser races were conducted in the morning, but as time drew near for the main attraction, excitement mounted, and the grounds surrounding the fort swarmed with a colorful but chaotic mass of stamping horses, noisy men, and wailing infants. An ominous note was added by the sudden appearance of 200 mounted and fully armed Navajos from the Canyon de Chelly. Called *ladrones* de Chelly, these were the renegades who had caused so much mischief over the past several years and who, even now, were outside the control of tribal leaders.

The Navajo entry, a nervous little sorrel pony, was owned by a huge fellow named Pistol Bullet, who stood six feet, four inches in his moccasins. He stalked about making last minute preparations and instructing the Indian lad who was to serve as his jockey. Dr. Kavenuagh moved among the men surrounding his thoroughbred and gave encouragement to Lieutenant Ortiz. The expectant throng formed in parallel lines along a track about 200 yards below the fort in front of the guard house. And the race was on.

As was the custom in New Mexico, horse races had no starter, the contestants themselves deciding the moment to begin. Three times the competing horses leaped forward, and in each instance the Indian rider turned them back, saying they had not started together. On the fourth try, the animals were given their heads and shot out neck and neck across the field. What happened next was not clear, even to the spectators, owing to the close-packed crowd and the boiling dust. Sergeant Nicholas Hodt, standing some distance away, said later, it appeared to him that Pistol Bullet's horse did not go a hundred yards before it ran off the track. "I could not see the cause of it," he stated, "but the report was that the Indian's bridle broke."

The other contestant, Ortiz, asserted that as soon as his thoroughbred began to pull ahead, the Navajo struck at his mount with a rope and deliberately swerved against him, and that in the collision that followed, the Indian boy was forced to the side while he raced on across the finish line. Whatever the circumstances, the Navajos were thrown into an uproar. Nor was the situation calmed by the action of the troopers, who gathered their winnings and paraded about the post grounds, playing fifes and fiddles and beating drums. The friendly atmosphere that preceded the race had completely evaporated, and in a few short moments, the air had become explosive.

The Indians withdrew to their camp in a surly mood, where several of them soon became drunk. Many were ready to believe their horse's bridle had been tampered with and they were victims of a fraud. Miguelito and other chiefs, who had worked hard in recent months to nurse the armistice, hoped to avoid an open rupture and they went among the people with soothing words. Even with this the *ladrones* would not be mollified. They had come out of their stronghold looking for a fight, and here was a situation ready-made for their purpose. The renegades broke into two parties—the larger moving up to the guard house, and a smaller band slipping away toward the garrison horse herd pastured in the valley.

As the *ladrones* approached the fort, they were challenged by a sentry and almost immediately unleashed a volley of arrows and bullets. The Officer of the Guard hurried up with reinforcements and fired into the howling mob, killing twelve. The remainder then fled back toward their camp. The outbreak of shooting aroused the post, and every man ran to arm himself. In the confusion, officers found it impossible to assemble their companies and some of the enlisted men began firing indiscriminately toward the Indians. Manuel managed to locate Lieutenant José María Sanches and detailed him to take twelve Mounted Volunteers and thirty-two infantry and go to the relief of the men holding the horse herd.

By the time Sanches came up with his force, the *ladrones* had wounded a Mexican herder and were endeavoring to drive the animals out of the west end of the valley. A fight ensued in which the soldiers recovered all but five horses, a mule, and two oxen. But they did succeed in capturing seven Indian horses. As the Navajos escaped, they chanced upon a military express rider about ten miles from the fort, took his horse and mailbag, and shot him in the arm.

In addition to the dozen Indians killed, more than a hundred were taken prisoner. Three of the latter, two men and a woman suffering from wounds, were treated in the post hospital. It was not immediately clear what effect the occurrence would have upon relations with the Navajo. Contact was reestablished with the chiefs who disclaimed responsibility for the outbreak, and on September 13 Manuel reported the particulars of the conflict "with deepest grief" to Colonel Canby in Santa Fe. Canby, understandably, was quite disturbed by the news, and he sent a request for more details, advising at the same time that he was transferring a company of Mounted Volunteers from Fort Union to help bolster Fauntleroy's defenses.[20]

During the following weeks, the Indians evidently posed no threat to the post's security. Manuel sent out routine patrols to check on Navajo activities, but the only thing they learned of interest concerned an encounter between this tribe and its old enemies, the Utes. On November 11, Colonel Chaves wrote to Canby in Santa Fe:

Sir: I have the honor to inform you of a fight which took place at Ojo del Gallo a short time since between the Ute & Navajo Indians, which resulted in the death of 4 Navajo and 10 taken Prisoners. Also the Navajo Indians suffered a loss of one hundred Horses.
Yours Respectfully, Very Obdt Serv
M Chaves
Lt Colonel 2nd Rgt. N.M.V.[21]

Shortly after this, on December 4, Manuel was relieved of his position and ordered to report to Albuquerque. Canby had been doing some quiet probing and was not satisfied that the circumstance surrounding the recent disturbance at Fort Fauntleroy had been fully explained. Apparently the practice of wagering government property had become known, and an examination of the books of the Quartermaster's Department at the fort revealed numerous irregularities. Added to this, conflicting reports of the horse race made determination of blame difficult, although it seemed that the commander, at the very least, had been lax in maintaining order.

When Manuel reached Albuquerque, he was met by Colonel Kit Carson, who explained that by Canby's orders he was to consider himself under arrest and confined to the limits of the town. However, Carson was authorized to "change the place of arrest to his home in the country [Ojuelos] subject to the same conditions as at Albuquerque."[22] Manuel expressed considerable dismay that his conduct was suspect and declared himself willing to cooperate fully in a preliminary investigation of the Navajo affair. Sometime afterward, the following exchange occurred between Manuel and Canby's aide, Lieutenant C. H. DeForrest:

DeForrest: When did you take command of the Fort?
Chaves: The 8th of August, 1861.
DeForrest: How long did you remain in command at this post?
Chaves: Until the beginning of November, 1861 [actually December].
DeForrest: During this time were you engaged in any expedition or scout outside the post?
Chaves: No sir.
DeForrest: During this time did anything occur at the post beyond the ordinary routine of post duties?
Chaves: . . . Yes sir. The Navajo Indians attacked the Fort. I don't recollect the day.
DeForrest: Relate the occurrences of that time.
Chaves: It commenced by Dr. Kavenaugh making up a horse race with some Navajos. After the race was over in which Dr. Kavenaugh was the winner, I and the Doctor retired into the Fort, when the Indians suddenly attacked the guard of the post. One of my men was wounded and 12 Indians were killed on the spot. I took 112 prisoners; the rest ran away. They were 500 in number.
DeForrest: What was the particular circumstance which led to this affair? The word or act.
Chaves: There was no cause given by us. I was in the house of Dr. Kavenaugh when the Indians attacked the guard.
DeForrest: How was the guard attacked?

Chaves: Shooting at them with rifles and arrows.

DeForrest: What reason if any did the Indians give for this attack?

Chaves: The chiefs who came in next day to speak to me said that they had nothing to do with it, but the *ladrones* of Canyon de Cha [Chelly] had done it.

DeForrest: For what purpose and by whose order were you relieved of command of the Fort?

Chaves: I was relieved by order of Colonel Canby to proceed to Albuquerque and await further orders.[23]

For the last weeks of December, Manuel remained in Albuquerque under nominal arrest. Other events in the territory attendant upon outbreak of the Civil War, however, were swiftly pushing his case into the background. His old unit, the Second New Mexico Mounted Volunteers, had been transferred, after his departure from Fort Fauntleroy, to duty at Fort Craig on the Rio Grande below Socorro. A Confederate army from Texas was swiftly moving up the river toward the New Mexican settlements, and a confrontation at Craig seemed imminent. In view of this, the officers, chaplain, and men of Manuel's regiment sent an urgent appeal to Colonel Canby, requesting that their commander be released and allowed to resume his position. Their petition read in part:

> The undersigned officers of the Volunteers and Militia of New Mexico would respectfully call your attention to the case of Lt. Col. Manuel Chaves, 2nd Regt. N. M. Vols., who has for two months been under arrest on unknown charges. For years past Lt. Col. Manuel Chaves has been well-known as a loyal citizen, an

> honorable man, and he has repeatedly proved himself a brave & efficient officer. In our opinion the cause in which we are all so deeply interested is every day losing the services of a man who is one of its strongest and ablest supporters.[24]

It is significant that the signature of C. Carson was appended at the end of the document to the list of men testifying to Manuel's good character. This petition, and perhaps other appeals on the accused's behalf, had the desired effect on Canby, and by a special order, dated January 21, 1862, he suspended the arrest of Manuel Chaves and directed him to report to the headquarters of his regiment.[25]

By February 10 Manuel had ridden the hundred miles of river road south from Albuquerque to Fort Craig. Here he found Colonel Canby with a handful of regular troops and about 3,000 untested New Mexican volunteers, tensely awaiting the approach of General H. H. Sibley's Confederate brigade. The need for a battle-experienced front line officer to help stiffen the backbone of the militia was clearly apparent and explains, in part, why Canby had moved with such swiftness to restore Manuel to his rank. So, once again the Little Lion was being drawn into a sequence of events that would prove a pivotal point in the history of the far Southwest.

General Edward R. S. Canby, Commander of Union forces in New Mexico during the Civil War. *Courtesy Museum of New Mexico.*

9

The Blue and the Gray on the Rio Grande

To most people the great issues of the Civil War were thrashed out on the battlefields of Antietam, Shiloh, Chancellorsville, Gettysburg, Chickamauga, and The Wilderness, and finally resolved at Appomattox Courthouse. Yet a small but significant part of the conflict unfolded in the vast and arid wasteland of the far Southwest.[1] As the Southern states began to leave the Union in the winter of 1860-1861, it was not clear whether New Mexico would remain loyal to the North or follow her neighbor Texas on the path of secession. A long-felt antipathy toward the Lone Star State, going back to the Texan-Santa Fe Expedition of 1841, and the virtual absence of Negro slavery along the upper Rio Grande would seemingly have been sufficient to keep New Mexico firmly loyalist. However, strong pro-southern sentiment was encouraged by several territorial newspapers and by many ex-Texans who had businesses and ranches around Mesilla. Moreover, Governor Abraham Rencher and other territorial officials, as well as officers of the regular army, were Southerners by birth and worked openly to push New Mexico into the Confederate ranks.

When war came in April 1861, a number of the highest ranking officers in New Mexico resigned from the United States Army and hurried home to offer their services to the South. Among them were Major Henry H. Sibley, last prewar commander of Fort Union, and two of Manuel's former superiors, Colonels Loring and Fauntleroy. Loring, who was abandoning his post as commander of Fort Marcy in Santa Fe, is reported to have called upon his old chief of scouts and asked him to join the Confederacy, promising him a colonel's commission in the Southern army. As recorded by Twitchell, Manuel Chaves declined the offer with these words: "Colonel, when I took the oath of allegiance to the United States, I swore to protect the American flag, and if my services are needed I shall give them to the country of my adoption and her flag."[2] Not long after this, Manuel was assigned command of Fort Fauntleroy, the office probably being given to a volunteer because of the dearth of regular officers brought on by the numerous defections.

On August 1, just as Manuel was preparing to leave Albuquerque for his new duty at Fauntleroy, Lieutenant-Colonel John R. Baylor, having seized Mesilla with 300 mounted Texans, proclaimed the creation of the Confederate Territory of Arizona, consisting of those portions of New Mexico and Arizona lying south of the thirty-fourth parallel. Lorenzo Labadie, who happened to be in nearby Las Cruces on Indian Superintendency business, narrowly escaped a traditional Southern tar and feathering. Later in the year, General Sibley with three regiments of Texans marched up from El Paso to support Baylor and to prepare for an invasion of northern New Mexico. Driving him was the determination to conquer all the territory in order that it

I Manuel Chaves Lieutenant Colonel. of the 2^c Regiment of N M Volunteers

do solemnly swear that I will bear true faith and allegiance to the United States of America, and that I will serve them honestly and faithfully against all their enemies and opposers whatsoever; and observe and obey the orders of the President of the United States, and the orders of the officers appointed over me, according to the Rules and Articles for the government of the Armies of the United States.

Sworn and subscribed to this 1st. day of August. A.D. 1861.

before me

C B Clark
Not. Public

Manuel Chaves.
Teniente Coronel del 2º Regº de Volunt. de N. M.

Oath of Allegiance signed by Manuel Chaves at the beginning of the Civil War in New Mexico, August 1, 1861. *Photo from the National Archives.*

might serve as a Confederate springboard for attacks on the gold fields of Colorado and California. But blocking his way was a Federal force of mixed regulars and volunteers collected by Colonel Canby at Fort Craig, midway up the Rio Grande.

Canby's position was not an enviable one. To protect his department, he had less than a thousand regulars—even these would have been withdrawn for service in the East had he not protested vigorously—and several regiments of militia, one led by Colonel Kit Carson, another by Colonel Miguel Pino and Lieutenant-Colonel Manuel Chaves.[3] Although a few of the volunteers, such as Manuel's brother Captain Román Baca and his cousin Lieutenant-Colonel J. Francisco Chaves, were hard-bitten campaigners who had won their spurs in the Indian wars, the majority were simple peon farmers, swiftly pressed into service for the emergency and deficient in both training and experience. For this reason, Canby hoped either to stay behind the protective walls of Fort Craig, or, if lured outside, to choose the ground for a battle.

During the second week of August, the Confederates approached the fort located on the west side of the Rio Grande, but fearing it too strong to storm, they decided to cross to the east bank of the river and proceed on to Albuquerque and Santa Fe. Canby assumed that the enemy intended to occupy a bluff overlooking both the river and the fort, and to forestall such a possibility, he dispatched Carson, Pino, and Chaves with their regiments to secure that strategic point. The native troops held the position through the night of February 19 and into the succeeding morning.

General Sibley and his Southerners moved around to Valverde ford a few miles north of Craig, by which time

Canby realized he was being bypassed, and he ordered out his troops. A brief engagement was fought on the evening of February 20, but the real test of strength awaited the following day. Skirmishing developed near the ford during the morning hours, and by mid-afternoon Canby had deployed his men over the Valverde field in preparation for an assault on the Confederate position. One end of the Union line was pegged down by a battery of artillery commanded by Captain Alexander McRae, and supporting it as a reserve was Pino and Chaves's regiment of militia.

The battle, when joined, was savagely fought. The Confederates, with only ten days rations remaining, needed a swift victory to keep their campaign in motion, and this knowledge summoned the utmost in bravery from their ranks. When Colonel Canby saw that his foe had taken the initiative and formed for an attack, he sent hasty word to Pino to be ready to support the artillery. But as the rebels charged the line, firing double-barreled shotguns and giving their famous yell, the native troops broke and fled in wild disorder. Canby dismounted and with Pino, Chaves, and other officers attempted to stem the tide. The panic, however, spread to some of the regulars, and nothing could be done to restore order among the terror-stricken men. The artillery was lost, and Captain McRae died gallantly at his post. Although other wings of the Union line fared better, the Colonel now ordered a general retreat to Craig, anticipating that an assault on the fort would soon follow.[4]

General Sibley, notwithstanding his victory on the field, was still feeling the strain of short supplies, and so leaving Canby's soldiers bottled up at Fort Craig, he marched hastily toward Albuquerque. In assessing his defeat at Valverde, Canby laid blame, perhaps excessively, upon the volunteers for failing to hold fast and come to the aid of the lamented Captain McRae. For the officers, however, he had only words of praise. In his official report of the battle, he declared, "Colonels Pino and Carson, Lieut. Cols. J. F. [José Francisco] Chaves and Manuel Chaves, and many other officers of the New Mexican Volunteers were noted for their zeal and energy."[5]

Several days after the battle of Valverde, Colonel Canby ordered Manuel to take the remnant of his volunteers, a mere sixty-six men, get ahead of the enemy, and join the Union forces preparing to defend the north. Swinging wide of the river on the west, Manuel rode through the foothills of the San Mateo[6] and Magdalena Mountains until he was opposite the village of Socorro. From a spy sent into the town, he learned that Nicolás Pino, Miguel's brother, heading a militia detachment, had surrendered to the Confederates to avoid bombardment of the civilian population. With this news he plunged on again toward Albuquerque, where he reported to Colonel Perea, who was in command of the few volunteers at that post.[7] Manuel says, "I remained there two days until the enemy came to Los Lunas [twenty miles below Albuquerque], receiving this information through a brother of mine who was amongst the Texans acting as my spy."[8] The brother surely was Román Bacá.

The quartermaster in charge of the Union supply depot in Albuquerque was Captain Herbert M. Enos. When he learned that an advance troop of Sibley's brigade was pressing up from the south, he collected what military stores he could carry and set fire to the remainder to avoid having them fall into Confederate hands. But many of the natives of the town, observing with undisguised anguish the destruction of so many useful goods rushed into the flames and rescued molasses, vinegar, soap, saddles, tools, and even office furniture. With his loaded wagons and escorted by volunteers under Colonel Perea and Lt. Colonel Chaves, Captain Enos fled toward Santa Fe.[9]

The cloud of black smoke billowing above Albuquerque was a disheartening beacon to Sibley's men. They had been counting heavily on the seizure of food, clothing, and munitions to replenish their depleted stores, without which their advance must inevitably grind to a halt. Scarcely had they occupied the town, however, when a friendly rider galloped in from the post of Cubero sixty miles to the west bearing a welcome message from staunch Confederate Dr. F. E. Kavenaugh. When Fort Fauntleroy was abandoned and its garrison transferred to Craig shortly before the Valverde action, Dr. Kavenaugh had closed his sutler's store and moved to Cubero, where resided a Union supply depot filled with war materiel originally intended for use against the Navajo. The doctor and three fellow Southerners in a bold bluff convinced the small volunteer guard to surrender, this coup netting the Confederates twenty-five wagon loads of commissary good, sixty arms, and 3,000 rounds of ammunition.[10] Thus providentially supplied, Sibley was able to continue his march against Santa Fe.[11]

On March 3, Manuel arrived in the capital with the wagon train of Captain Enos. Immediately he reported to Major James L. Donaldson, then commanding the 200 regulars stationed there. Donaldson had already decided that he could not defend Santa Fe, and he directed Colonel Chaves to assemble whatever he could find in the way of volunteers and be prepared to join a general retreat eastward. At nine o'clock on the following morning, after putting two warehouses of stores to the torch, the Union troops, along with the new and loyal territorial governor and other civil officials, evacuated the capital and took the road through Apache Canyon toward Fort Union. Manuel, with a meager handful of militiamen, marched in the wake of the cavalcade as part of a protective escort for the wagons. But, as historian Martin Hall points out, "By the time the column had reached Fort Union, all the natives, except Colonel Chaves and a few of his officers, had deserted along the way."[12]

Since the beginning of the Confederate invasion, the New Mexicans had shown themselves apathetic toward the issues of the war, and this, coupled with their inborn fear of Texans, rendered most of them something less than dedicated soldiers. With the coming of March, every native farmer's attention turned toward the preparation of his fields for spring planting, and with no formal leave-taking, those few still bearing arms simply departed for their homes and families. Thus the steadfastness of Manuel Chaves to the Union cause throughout the dark days of defeat appears all the more remarkable. Apparently, having pledged his loyalty, he intended to fight on to the end, whether his fellow countrymen joined him or not.

The issue in New Mexico, however, was fast approaching a climax. During the second week in March, Major Charles L. Pyron, who had assumed charge of the Confederate advance while Sibley remained in Albuquerque, entered Santa Fe and began unlimbering his men for a push toward strategic Fort Union. In the meantime, a body of Colorado volunteers, parading under the name "Pike's Peakers," had descended from Denver to augment the slender garrison at Union in hopes of staving off an attack on their own territory. Manuel Chaves and a troop of these Coloradoans led by Major John M. Chivington rode west, encamping at the village of San José on the Pecos River. From this point, Manuel took six soldiers and scouted all the way to Santa Fe. According to his own testimony, he slipped inside the capital, made contact with Padre José Manuel

Gallegos, learned what he could of Confederate strength and plans, and made a hasty report to Chivington.[13]

Evidently the major, who had a shade more than 400 infantry and cavalry, planned to drive as far as the capital, but from Manuel he learned that the enemy was moving into Apache Canyon toward the summit of Glorieta Pass. Hastening forward, Chivington engaged the Confederate advance in a sharp battle on the afternoon of March 26, and then retired to wait for the main contingent of regular and volunteer forces under Colonel John P. Slough, which was marching down from Fort Union in support.

In the predawn of the 28th, Chivington and Slough united and immediately arranged strategy for what they hoped would be a decisive conflict in their favor. The plan called for Slough to move ahead with the main body of the army and test Confederate defenses in the pass, while Chivington and his men attempted to gain the enemy rear by a clandestine ride over Glorieta Mesa. But the major from Colorado was unfamiliar with the New Mexican terrain, and the success of his flanking maneuver depended upon finding a trustworthy scout to guide him along the forest trails on the mesa. Who better than Colonel Manuel Chaves, whose mission to Santa Fe had already won Chivington's respect. To Manuel, the country along the Santa Fe Trail surrounding Glorieta Pass and the Upper Pecos River was as familiar as his backyard at Ojuelos. Here, twenty years before, he had held a position of command in Armijo's army that humbled the Texan-Santa Fe Expedition, and how many times he traveled through the same area to his sheep operations in the Pecos Valley in years afterward remains a matter for speculation. Major Chivington may have had little choice in the matter, but as subsequent events proved, Colonel Chaves was the right man for the job.

With some 900 men and the artillery, Colonel Slough penetrated Glorieta Pass, and near Pigeon's Ranch, a famous hostelry on the Santa Fe Trail, collided with the Confederates. The ground was hotly contested throughout the day, until both sides paused in exhaustion, but it was the Southerners who held the field as evening came. During the engagement, Slough had anticipated moment by moment that Chivington would sweep down off the mesa to the south and strike the enemy in the flank. But the major, his guide, and troops failed to appear.

Far from having lost his way, Manuel Chaves on the afternoon of the 28th led Chivington's force straight to the soft underbelly of the Confederate army. When the men emerged from the pine and piñon forest, they were on the rocky rim of Glorieta Mesa directly above the narrow exit to Apache Canyon. Manuel's first words to Chivington at this moment have been recorded and are perhaps remarkable for their directness and brevity. "You are right on top of them, Major."[14] And indeed they were.

Below on the flats outside the canyon rested sixty or more wagons comprising the enemy supply train and protected only by a single artillery piece and a handful of soldiers and teamsters. Even as they viewed the extraordinary opportunity open to them, the volunteers could hear the muffled booms of battle echoing from the pass several miles to the east. As Manuel stood on the ledge, his thoughts must have fled back to that August day in 1846, when under much different circumstances, he had threatened and pleaded with Governor Armijo to defend this same position against the advancing army of General Kearny.

After studying the scene for an hour, Chivington assigned command of the assault force to Captain William H. Lewis, while Manuel selected the best avenue leading down off the mesa. At the order, "In single file, double-quick, charge!" the men spilled over the rim and descended upon the dumbfounded Confederates. A scattering of small arms fire and several futile bursts from the cannon were all the resistance the defenders could muster, and within a short time, Chivington's "Pike's Peakers" had possession of the wagon train. Since nothing could be carried back over the steep trail, everything was set afire—according to Manuel's statement, sixty-one wagons and a carriage—and the artillery piece was spiked and tumbled down an arroyo.[15] Then, with considerable dispatch, the men regained the crest of the mesa.

Here Major Chivington had received word from a courier sent by Slough to rejoin the main army as speedily as possible. Chaves explained that to strike directly for the Union camp meant leaving the trail followed earlier in the day and taking to the ravines and brush, a responsibility he could not assume since night was fast approaching. At this point, a priest from the village of Pecos, Padre Ortiz, appeared on horseback and saluted the officers in Spanish. With Manuel translating, he offered to lead the regiment back over the mesa by a shorter route and warned that if the main trail was pursued, they would doubtless encounter Confederate patrols. Since Manuel knew and trusted the priest, he advised Chivington to accept his services, and thus with a clerical guide, the column was conducted safely to Slough's headquarters.[16]

As successive events revealed, Chivington's action at Apache Canyon broke the Confederate back in New Mexico. Loss of the supply train so dispirited the Southern leadership that within a matter of days a withdrawal down the Rio Grande toward Texas was begun. Strangely, the crucial, perhaps decisive, role played by Colonel Chaves in guiding the Colorado volunteers found little or no mention in the official military records concerning the pivotal battle at Glorieta Pass.[17] But the officers and men who had participated in Chivington's foray remembered what Manuel had done and in later years gave him ample credit for his part in the victory.[18]

After the action at Glorieta, the Northern forces retired eastward toward Fort Union. At the village of San José, Manuel received notice from Ojuelos that the Navajo had driven off one of his flocks numbering 11,000 sheep, and promptly, he says, "Colonel Slough granted me permission to go look to my interests."[19] After an absence of twelve days, during which nothing could be done to recover his loss, he returned to the theater of conflict and reported to Colonel Canby. Upon receiving news of the engagement at Glorieta, Canby had left Fort Craig and marched up the Rio Grande, intending to unite his troops with those from Fort Union. He encamped on the outskirts of Albuquerque on April 8, but after an exchange of cannon fire with the Confederate garrison, he abandoned hope of taking the town. Manuel arrived during the day and that night received word to march, as Canby had decided to lead his army through Carnuel Pass and Tijeras Canyon east of Albuquerque. Once through the pass, the soldiers continued northward along the slope of the Sandia Mountains to the village of San Antonio, where advance contingents of the Fort Union troops were encountered.

From here Manuel Chaves, along with his friend Colonel Miguel Pino, who had remained at Canby's side since Valverde, was ordered to return to Albuquerque and spy upon movements of the enemy. After determining that the veterans of the Glorieta fight had left Santa Fe and moved downriver to re-enforce the Albuquerque garrison, Chaves and Pino rode throughout the night and entered Canby's tent at six o'clock in the morning to advise him of their discovery. The Colonel, now that the Colorado volunteers and regulars from Fort Union had swelled his command, decided to retrace the route through Carnuel Pass and engage the rebels. Unaware of the extent his foes had been crippled by the loss of supplies at Apache Canyon, he thought they would either attempt to hold Albuquerque or countermarch to Santa Fe. Thus, while he returned with the army by way of the pass, Canby instructed Manuel to swing around the north end of the Sandias, strike the Rio Grande, and find out if the Confederates showed signs of moving toward the capital again.

Manuel reached the river at night near the village of Algodones, where he took two Texans prisoner. Apparently from them he learned that Sibley not only had given up hope of reoccupying Santa Fe, but had already started a general withdrawal down the Rio Grande toward Mesilla. The following day, Manuel hurried south, passed through Albuquerque, and caught up with Canby's pursuing force near Peralta in time to participate in a sharp but indecisive skirmish with a wing of Sibley's brigade.[20] This small engagement took place on April 15, and during the next several days the two armies, the Blue on the east bank, the Gray on the west, traveled south along the river within sight of one another. The Confederates were obviously in full flight, and as long as this was the case, Canby had no wish to expose his men to needless risk. Nor did he wish to capture Sibley's command, which he could have probably done easily, and be forced to feed and care for huge numbers of prisoners.

General Sibley had hoped to salvage something from his

retreat by attacking and burning Fort Craig, which he knew was defended by a skeleton garrison of volunteers under Kit Carson. But with Canby's relentless pursuit, he realized any such attempt would be foolhardy, and he concentrated his whole attention on moving the brigade out of New Mexico as swiftly as possible. At the junction of the Puerco and Rio Grande above Socorro, Sibley went into camp in full view of Canby's men on the opposite shore. During the night, however, he roused his exhausted and footsore troops, loaded a few provisions on pack mules, and slipped away by a trail that led around the west side of the Magdalena and San Mateo Mountains. In taking this route, he escaped the watchful eye of the Union army, avoided Fort Craig, and reached Mesilla undisturbed. Colonel Canby, convinced that the Confederates could cause no more harm, was content to let them flee. On the morning he observed their departure from the river, he sent Manuel Chaves to collect the wagons and supplies abandoned near the mouth of the Puerco and move them to the town of Sabinal, while he continued on to Fort Craig.

Two days later Manuel arrived at Craig and was shortly placed under arrest. According to allegations made at the time, he had, in disobedience of orders, taken the salvaged wagons to La Joya instead of Sabinal, where he disposed of them for his own profit.[21] Although no formal charges were prepared, Canby issued the arrest order until an investigation could be made. Throughout the end of April and the first weeks of May, Manuel remained subject to this order, although he was not confined. Canby soon went to Albuquerque, after placing Colonel Gabriel R. Paul in charge of Fort Craig. To him Manuel applied for permission to leave the post and attend affairs at Ojuelos. When license was granted, verbally by Colonel Paul and

Kit Carson, scout, Indian Agent, Commander of New Mexican Militia, and friend of Manuel Chaves. *Courtesy Museum of New Mexico.*

in the presence of Kit Carson and Miguel Pino, Manuel rode the forty miles to his ranch, and for the next eighteen days enjoyed a leisurely visit with his family. But at the end of that time, he received a curt message from Colonel Canby demanding to know why he had left Fort Craig in violation of his arrest and directing him to report to headquarters in Albuquerque at once.[22]

Arriving in Albuquerque, Manuel was able to convince Canby that his absence from Fort Craig had been approved by Colonel Paul, but by this time he may have gained the unpleasant feeling the commandant was hounding him. On March 23, he learned that a General Court Martial had convened several days before in the town of Polvadera above Fort Craig and that his presence there was demanded. Manuel's old comrade Kit Carson had been named president of the court, but evidently before he could assume his duty, the body met in preliminary session, judged that there were no grounds for subjecting Lt. Colonel Chaves to trial, and, upon approval of Canby, who had just been promoted to brigadier-general, dissolved itself.[23] The following July another court met in Peralta, but it too adjourned, in Manuel's words, "for want of charges against me."[24]

This entire incident is extremely mystifying. Throughout the initial proceedings, Manuel showed himself not only willing to cooperate in an investigation but hopeful that specific charges would be made so that he could answer them. Unfortunately, since documents are incomplete or sparing in detail, the accusations against him, regarding the violation of orders and disposal of the Confederate wagons, are vague, and we can only assume that his conduct, if it ran counter to Canby's command, was the result of a misunderstanding rather than criminal intent. The courts must have reached the same conclusion, for no evidence sufficient to warrant a trial could be produced. Also bearing weight in Manuel's favor must have been the now well known fact expressed by one of the investigating officers, Captain A. W. Evans, "that the services of Lt. Col. M. Chaves in the affair at Apache Cañon were of the most valuable character to the Union."[25]

The strife and turmoil experienced by New Mexico during the Civil War temporarily obscured the older, abiding Indian problem that plagued the territory. But with the end of Union-Confederate hostilities, citizen and soldier alike again turned to the challenge posed by the Indians. As mentioned, shortly after the battle of Glorieta, Manuel received an urgent call to come to Ojuelos, where the Navajo had just made off with one of his flocks. With his discharge from service, he returned home for good and found the Indians had virtually stripped his ranch of livestock, including 30,000 sheep and all cattle and horses.[26] With his brother-in-law Lorenzo, who had a substantial interest in these ranching activities, he subsequently entered a claim against the government. But a bill for their relief was not introduced into Congress until 1876, and not finally approved until after Manuel's death.[27]

After totaling his losses, Chaves decided against restocking the hacienda; instead, he transferred his operations eastward to the Pecos River where, with personal direction, he hoped to build up smaller flocks and herds that he and Lorenzo had maintained there for a decade or more. Influencing this move was the fact that Lorenzo, who had recently become the Indian agent at the Fort Sumner Reservation located along the middle Pecos, would be available to assist in the business; also, the military would provide a ready market for mutton and beef. Before closing Ojuelos, however, Manuel received an urgent appeal for aid from settlers living in the valley near Socorro.

A large Navajo war party, numbering more than a

hundred, had struck several ranches, killing shepherds, seizing a huge quantity of stock, and carrying away the young son of Matías Contreras, one of the most distinguished residents of the district. Gathering eight of his own men, including Román Sanches and José María Chaves, Manuel rode to the Contreras hacienda where he was joined by the owner, another rancher, Don Tomás Baca, and four vaqueros.[28] A rider was sent to Fort Craig for reinforcements, but Matías Contreras, distraught over the loss of his son, insisted that the party start at once, without waiting for the soldiers.

Manuel guided his companions away from the Rio Grande and over a seared plain above the Magdalena Mountains. Turning south he moved into the foothills of the San Mateos and approached the Ojo de la Monica or Monica Spring, having covered almost a hundred miles in less than two days. Here he was on familiar ground, since this was some of the same country he had ridden when scouting for Colonel Loring's Gila Expedition in 1857.

The pursuers, all mounted on mules, pushed their animals hard as the freshness of the broad trail they were following showed the Indians were near. Not far from the Ojo de la Monica, they ran with a jar into the Navajo rear guard. Perhaps Manuel had hoped the surprise appearance of his band would stampede the Indians into flight, or maybe he merely intended to harry them and slow down their progress with the stolen sheep until relief from Fort Craig arrived. But the Navajos, on the edge of their own country and viewing the small number of New Mexicans, neither panicked nor abandoned their spoils. Instead, they wheeled their horses around, formed a skirmishing line, and sensing an easy conquest over old foes, gave vent to war cries and victory yells.

Grasping the seriousness of the situation, Manuel dismounted his men, directed them to tie their mules somewhat to the rear, and to take cover in a scattering of juniper trees. Immediately Navajo sharpshooters flanked the position and in a matter of minutes brought down all the mules. For Manuel Chaves, the future at this moment must have looked as dim as it had on that day more than thirty years before when he and the Cebolletan youths had been surrounded on the lip of Canyon de Chelly.

Throughout the afternoon and early evening, the usual serenity of Monica Spring was trespassed by the violence and smoke of battle. Manuel slipped from man to man offering encouragement and occasionally, because of his superior marksmanship, firing their rifles while they loaded his single-shot Hawkins. Around his neck he wore a red tie that made him a conspicuous target for the Indians, but in spite of the urgings of his comrades, and perhaps with a show of bravado, he refused to remove it. José María Chaves sustained several wounds, yet continued discharging his weapon until felled by a shot through the head. Román Sanches died, as did most of the others in succession. By dark Manuel, who, except for two bullets through his hat, had escaped unscathed, was left with only Matías Contreras and Tomás Baca. The latter had suffered a severe wound that shattered his lower leg, and under cover of night his two companions dragged him to a sheltered spot on a hillside. When dawn neared with the bleak prospect of renewed fighting, Manuel took stock of his ammunition and found three bullets remaining in his shot pouch. During the clash of the previous day, he had fired eighty times and knew that his sure aim had taken its toll. The Navajos, in fact, had lost interest in facing the old Hawkins again, and as the flames of sunrise swept across the gray hearth of the New Mexican sky, Manuel surveyed the land below and found the Indians gone.

Contriving a crude litter, he and Contreras bore the feverish Tomás Baca along their back trail toward the Rio Grande. During the day, they encountered the soldiers from Fort Craig led by Captain Román Baca. Hearing that his brother was chasing a superior party of Navajos and fearing for his safety, Baca had driven his men in haste. Arriving too late for the battle, his appearance on the trail was welcome nonetheless. Tomás Baca, although losing his leg, survived the ordeal and lived long in Socorro County. Matías Contreras, who was able to ransom his son some months afterward, later served in the territorial legislature. Of the memorable contest at Ojo de la Monica, Manuel Chaves always claimed it was his greatest fight. Giving credit to his foes, he declared that the Navajos, well armed with rifles, displayed lofty courage, and had his own men showed any less, none would have lived to bear the tale.[29]

But the war days of the Navajo were numbered. General James H. Carleton, Canby's successor as military commandant of New Mexico, was grimly determined to exterminate or capture the Indians, who, during the later part of 1862, had killed sixty-two persons, wounded thirty-four, and stolen livestock valued at $340,000. In pursuit of his aggressive policy, he sent Kit Carson, now Colonel of the First New Mexico Cavalry, to subdue the Mescalero Apache, long the scourge of the southern half of the territory. The task was completed by January 1863, and the Mescalero were moved to the Bosque Redondo Reservation at Fort Sumner on the Pecos. Lorenzo Labadie became the tribal agent. Next, Carson was sent after the Navajo, and although he engaged in no major battles, the Indians' homeland was ravaged, their fields burned, their livestock destroyed. By the summer of 1864, destitute bands totaling 8,000 people had come in and surrendered. These were taken east on a forced march and also placed at Bosque Redondo, adjacent to their traditional Apache enemies.[30]

Next to nothing is known of Manuel's activities during his years of ranching on the Pecos. As long as the Navajo and Apache were held at Bosque Redondo, he must have enjoyed some prosperity, selling sheep to the agency and the military establishment. Lorenzo's job, as it turned out, was scarcely enviable. His jurisdiction extended only to the Mescalero, the Navajo being considered prisoners of war and subject solely to the military. Conflicts of authority were frequent and Agent Labadie often provoked the officers at Fort Sumner by doggedly pursuing a policy of fair treatment for his charges. Repeatedly he urged removal of the Navajo to another reservation to avoid conflict with his Apaches and because Bosque Redondo was simply too small to support both tribes. But nothing was done, and by 1866, the Mescalero had slipped away from the reservation and gone to shifting for themselves. Two years later, the Navajo, after delivering promises of good conduct, were allowed to return to their old homeland in western New Mexico and Arizona, and Bosque Redondo was closed. Lorenzo, freed from his burdensome duty, joined Manuel at the ranch located near the village of Puerto de Luna and remained there for the remainder of his days.[31]

During the late 1860s and early 1870s, Manuel Chaves enjoyed, perhaps for the first time in his life, a period relatively free from combat. To be sure, there were occasional thefts of his livestock by stray bands of Plains Indians or Apaches from the south, but the era of raiding was nearly done. And well it was, for in his threescore years, Manuel had suffered his share of wounds, and with advancing

Ceremonial sword and "Chihuahua style" silver inlay spur of Manuel Chaves. Now in possession of Amado Chaves Summers, Santa Fe. *Author photo.*

age their effects produced longer and longer bouts of unrelieved pain. He continued to make frequent trips to Santa Fe to care for business affairs and visit with old friends, particularly his comrade of many trails, Miguel Pino. In 1874 he finally sold the house behind Guadalupe Chapel and at the same time may have closed out any mercantile interests remaining.[32]

In his declining years, Manuel seemed ready to devote the strength lingering in him to developing the land and raising stock. But one part of his life's work was still undone. Since boyhood there had abided with him the persistent memory of an oak grove beyond the San Mateo Peaks, where, in flight from the Navajo, he had rested in agony, nursed his arrow wounds, and perhaps discovered the firm temper of his iron will and stamina. For him, life's circle would not properly close until he returned and claimed the soil that had received the blood of his youth. It would be a homecoming, a statement of his constant triumph over hardship, and, at last, a place to root his family and experience a measure of peace. The Pecos River ranch offered a livelihood, but nothing more, and it would have to be left behind, for the crenelated peaks and vaulting ridges of western New Mexico beckoned with their magic promise to an old man, now bearded and crippled. So Manuel Chaves listened to the call in his blood and resolved to build again.

10
San Mateo

The military campaign against the Navajo led by Kit Carson during the winter of 1863-1864 brought to a close two centuries of warfare between that tribe and the New Mexicans. Carson's marches and countermarches through the Indian province had been supported by smaller expeditions of native militia, one of which was directed by Román Baca in November of 1863. With a party of 116 residents of Cebolleta, Baca traveled in a northwesterly direction for six days and close to the Chusca Mountains engaged 200 Navajos, killing six and capturing three.[1] The evidence suggests that on returning from this foray, he scouted the country west of the San Mateo Peaks with the intention of finding a suitable site for a ranch. Certainly it was not mere chance that he selected a well-watered location near the oak grove where his brother Manuel had always planned to return. We may guess that Manuel Chaves had spoken often of the episode in his youth that had led him to rest beneath these trees, and of his determination to claim that spot one day.

It was probably in the following year that Román Baca came back with several score Cebolletans and founded the village of San Mateo along the shoulders of a small creek that issued from the mountains on the east. To the Indians, this place had been known as The Meadows, because the shallow water table nourished acres of rich grassland, and the new settlers found it ideal ground for a farming and ranching enterprise. With the bulk of the Navajo safely removed to Bosque Redondo in eastern New Mexico, homes could be built, a church reared, *acequias* dug, and fields turned without the constant demand of vigilance and caution that had attended such work in the past.

Román moved east a mile or so and laid the foundations for his hacienda not far from a copious spring. Within time he built an immense manor house to shelter his wife, Ramona Labadie, four children, and a crowd of servants and herders. Near the dwelling and enclosed by a protective rock wall grew an apple orchard, the saplings imported from Mexico, while shading the entrance to the hacienda was a cluster of gnarled cottonwoods.

Once, in later years, a Mormon, who owned a number of mules and scrapers, was working on the construction of the Santa Fe Railroad in western New Mexico. After a falling out with his employer, he started home for Utah with a family of several wives and equipment, when he stopped for the night at the Baca hacienda. Needing supplies and grain for the animals, he arranged with Román to perform a little excavation work; driving his wives with the same whip he used for his mules, he dug a large stock tank just south of the ranch house. Román summoned his people from San Mateo and admonished them to observe how the gringos worked their women. "Here is proof," he intoned, "that they are the devil's people."[2]

From what little is known of life on the hacienda, it appears Román Baca ruled his domain with heavy handed authority. Persons encroaching upon his grazing land were severely dealt with by hired gunmen, although travelers pausing overnight at the ranch were accorded the customary hospitality then typical of rural New Mexico. Frequently, wayfarers were drawn into a poker game with the genial host and invariably the following morning found themselves shorn of their fortunes. Rather than have his guests depart destitute, Román invited each to replenish his purse from a trunk near the main entrance containing silver coins. If the traveler was moderate in what he took, he proceeded on his journey undisturbed, but if he dipped into the trunk with obvious greed, Román dispatched a pair of Apache servants to indulge in a little brigandage on the road and retrieve the money.[3]

At the height of his ranching activity, Román had some 40,000 sheep grazing on his pastures and annually freighted large quantities of wool to St. Louis by ox team. But from the first, he had intended that Manuel should claim his share of this small empire, and over the years, while waiting for his brother, he carefully protected the oak grove that grew two miles north of his own home. At last, in 1876 Manuel Chaves, then in his mid-sixties, was ready to take up the challenge and sink his final roots in the San Mateo earth.

The years that followed were not easy ones. Carving out a new home on what was still a frontier, building a ranch, and caring for a large family—Manuel and Vicenta now had a total of eight children—was a task meant for a younger man.[4] But the old fire still burned, and with the aid of his eldest sons and with the firm support of Román the job was done.

Under the protecting canopy of his oaks, Manuel raised a mansion of adobe and stone; if it could be described as sumptuous, it was only so for its time and place. Charles Lummis, who visited there in the late 1880s, took pains to record "the domestic and social life of the New Mexican uppercrust as he saw it in the charming house of old Don Manuel Chaves."

> The *casa* is a roomy and finely built adobe, divided by a hall twelve feet wide running from east to west. The rooms are large and well-lighted, tastefully furnished in American style, handsomely papered and carpeted. The windows are hung with lace curtains, while the rugs and table-covers are precious Navajo blankets. Heat is furnished by the delightful corner fireplaces peculiar to the New Mexicans, and unequaled by any sort in the world. Pictures, mirrors, and various knick-nacks complete the pleasant picture. This comfortably appointed house was as unlike my native New England homestead as possible in all but one thing—that it was *home*; and home not only for its people, but for their guests.[5]

In the center of the great house was an open patio containing a hand-dug well and beehive-shaped adobe ovens where Indian women did the family washing and baking. Several of these servants had been taken from their tribes as children and knew no other life than that of the Chaves household. One of them, Lupe, seized in a battle with the Comanches when she was only three, continued to serve Manuel's son Amado well into the twentieth century.[6]

Behind the main house were workrooms, quarters for the help, and a blacksmith shop. For a brief time the ranch was a regular stage stop on the Santa Fe to Fort

Placita or interior courtyard of the Manuel Chaves hacienda at San Mateo, 1888. Note round adobe ovens at left. In the background, its window bisected by the roof ladder, can be seen a portion of the chapel built by Manuel. *Charles Lummis photo.*

Wingate route, the coach receiving minor repairs from the blacksmith and the passengers sampling Chaves hospitality. On one occasion, Manuel placed his son Irineo on the stage going east. The boy had a liberally supplied wallet and instructions on making his way to a school in St. Louis. Before boarding the coach, he received a firm handshake from his father and a tearful reminder from his mother to pay strict attention to his religious duties. The road led north to El Dado stage station, then east to Cabezon, and finally to Bernalillo on the Rio Grande, where the aspiring student was supposed to transfer to another line and proceed on his journey. But Bernalillo was as far as he got.

Coming from the backwoods of western New Mexico, Irineo decided he lacked proper clothes for a young man about to enter the big city. And here he thought to outfit himself in proper style. First he entered the dry goods store of a Jewish merchant and purchased an enormous suitcase, then he set out to locate a shop that could furnish him correct attire. While prowling along main street's row of businesses, he spied a gambling hall and heard from within the noise of the monte tables. Probably no New Mexican youth of this period could have resisted similar temptation, and through the doors of the hall he disappeared, as a lamb to the slaughter. When he emerged an hour later, it was with panic in his heart, for with separation from his money, he was left without means to continue his trip. Lacking even funds for a stage ticket home, his first thought was to regain the money for his suitcase. But the merchant would not hear of a refund, and there Irineo stood, with empty pockets and an empty bag.

In utter despair he walked down along the Rio Grande and sat beneath some cottonwoods overhanging the river's edge. But thoughtful contemplation sometimes shows the way out of a dilemma, and this was one of those occasions. Irineo jumped up and began collecting round, smooth stones on the shore, which he filed away in his suitcase. Closing the lid and finding that the contents rattled, he went about pulling up cottonwood withes by their roots, and these he used as stuffing to tighten the load.

Later, when the westbound coach prepared to depart from Bernalillo station, Irineo was there with his murderously heavy suitcase. "I have no money for a ticket," he explained to the agent, "but when we arrive at my home, my father Don Manuel Chaves will pay the charges. And as security, here is my bag filled with new clothes."

The driver hefted the suitcase into the boot of the stage, Irineo climbed in, and the mules leaned into their traces and headed west. After his initial surprise subsided, Don Manuel, indeed, paid his son's stage fare. But his astonishment increased as Irineo opened his new bag and displayed what he carried. Taking up the cottonwood shoots, the old Indian fighter examined them critically and then announced with emphasis, "You brought them. Now you plant them!"

And plant them Irineo did, relieved that his folly had provoked no greater storm. The withes took root in front of the Chaves house and within time formed a magnificent cottonwood grove, overshadowing the neighboring oaks. The details of the story were soon common knowledge throughout the neighborhood, and the people of San Mateo thereafter referred to the great trees as "Don Irineo's education."[7]

From the beginning of the development of his new ranch, Manuel relied heavily upon Amado's talent and strength. The eldest son had gone to Santa Fe in 1864, at the time the rest of the family was moving from Ojuelos to the Pecos, and there received his secondary education at San Miguel College. During his years of attendance, he resided in the house of his godfather Don Miguel Pino, from whom he must have learned details of the youthful exploits of his own father.[8] Upon graduation, Amado went to Washington, D.C. to continue his studies, receiving a law degree from the National University in 1876. He apparently remained in the capital a short time, serving at a post in the Department of Interior, but a call from Manuel soon brought him to the hacienda at San Mateo.[9]

Amado established a part-time law practice in Santa Fe, but during the lambing and shearing season and other important work periods with the stock, he was at the ranch superintending these operations. While in Washington, he had investigated the possibility of importing a finer grade of sheep and goat to New Mexico. His father and other raisers had always stocked their pastures with a small, tough sheep of Merino breeding called Charro, essentially the same animal brought to the Southwest by colonizer Juan de Oñate in 1598. Although able to multiply on sparse desert graze, these sheep produced inferior quantities of wool and meat. Regarding Amado's efforts to upgrade the industry, the *Daily New Mexican* reported to its readers in the spring of 1876: "We have received a fine sample of Angora mohair and Merino wool that will be introduced into New Mexico this summer by Señor Amado Chaves, who is now in Washington. The fleece measures twelve inches in length, is firm, white, and of fine quality. It would pay those who are interested to come by the New Mexican office and see the same on exhibit."[10]

Through the late 1870s and early 1880s, both Manuel and Román expanded the territorial limits of their range with the acquisition of neighboring land grants, whose antecedents extended back to colonial times. The most important of these was the Fernández Grant, originally

Román Antonio Baca, brother of Manuel Chaves. *Courtesy Museum of New Mexico.*

Amado Chaves, eldest son of Manuel Chaves. *Photo courtesy Consuelo Chaves Summers.*

San Miguel, a sheep camp on the Chaves ranch near San Mateo, 1888. *Charles Lummis photo.*

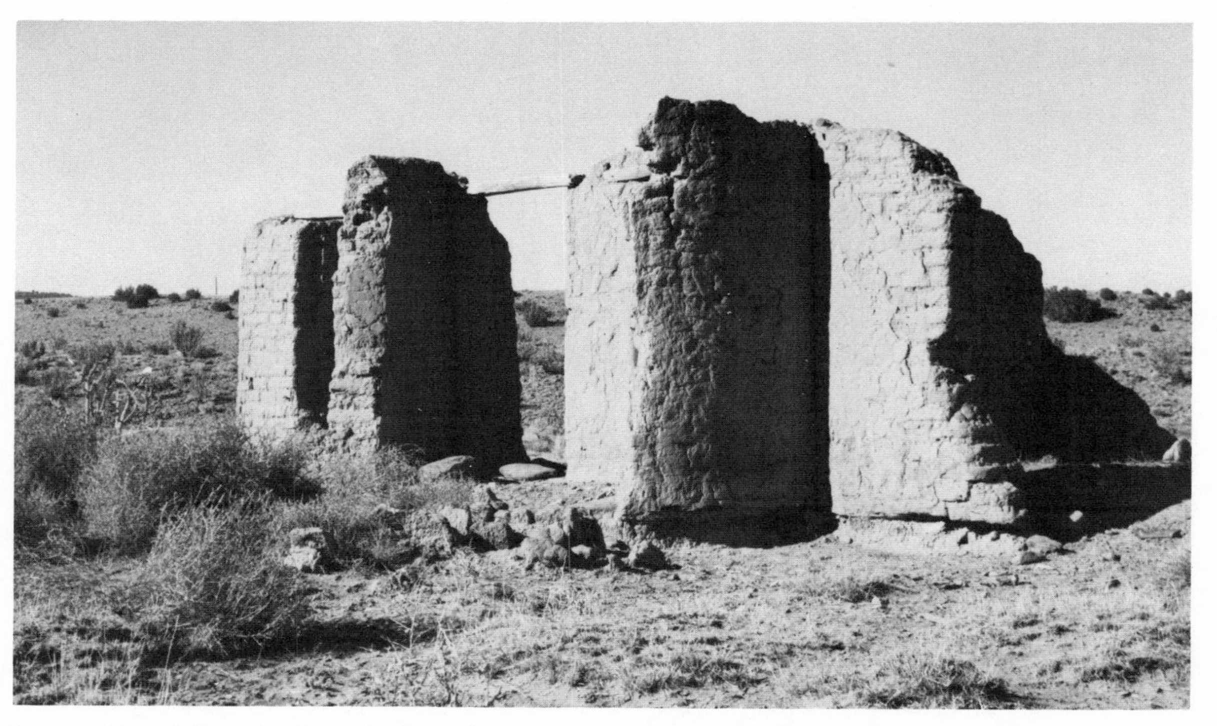

Ruins of San Miguel today. *Author photo.*

A portion of Manuel Chaves' flocks at the San Mateo ranch, 1888. *Charles Lummis photo.*

conveyed by the Spanish governor in 1767 to Bartolomé Fernández de la Pedrera.[11] Titles to some of these lands, guaranteed under the Treaty of Guadalupe Hidalgo ending the Mexican War, were still in the process of being confirmed by the Federal government, and Amado was obliged to make several trips to Washington to support personally the interests of his family. An idea of his progress can be gained from this local newspaper report in 1882: "Amado Chaves, Esq., while in Washington, attended to the interests of the owners of the Cebolleta Grant in Valencia County, and met with much success, obtaining after some hard work at the Departments of Interior and Justice, the patent for the grant. The area of the grant is over two hundred thousand acres, and it is well watered and finely timbered. Don Román A. Baca of San Mateo is one of the principal owners."[12]

Amado's schedule was temporarily interrupted in late summer of 1882 when he suffered a severe attack of malarial fever while attending business in Santa Fe. Confined in the hospital there for several weeks, his father and uncle Román rode up on the Santa Fe Railway from the ranch to cheer him on to recovery. What must have been Manuel's thoughts as he traveled the rails in relative comfort over the country where he had ridden and fought for so many decades! With population mushrooming and change sweeping the land, he may well have reflected upon the adventurous times that now were fast slipping away and been glad to have been a part of an epic and a way of life that would not be repeated.

In his last years Manuel Chaves entertained on at least two occasions at his San Mateo ranch the remarkable and energetic Charles Lummis. In the fall of 1884, Lummis set out from Cincinnati to walk 3,000 miles to a newspaper job awaiting for him in Los Angeles. As motive for going on foot, he declared, "I was young (twenty-six) with educated muscles and full experience of the pleasures of long pedestrian tours."[13] On the middle leg of his journey, he entered New Mexico, a part of the country then virtually unknown to easterners, and was at once captivated by the dark, brooding landscape, and by the equally dark but picturesque and hospitable inhabitants. As he hiked across the territory, sharing the hearths and campfires of the native people, he heard again and again of the legendary *Leoncito*, now aged, nearly blind, and burdened by old wounds but yet living and working on his hacienda at San Mateo. Some men are stirred by tales of heroism in others, and Lummis was one of these. As he reached Grants Station in western New Mexico, he swung off the main California road and took up the twenty-five mile trail that led to the Chaves ranch.

The reception, for a perfect stranger, he found somewhat overwhelming. "Talk about hospitality," he wrote later, "I have sampled a good many brands of the article in a good many different places, but I never found any ahead of that on tap at San Mateo. I was treated like a king. The best room in the place was mine. 'You are in your own house,' said Don Manuel to me, in a fashion which indicated that he meant it. And though the language of the household was alien to my ears, I was made as much at home as ever anywhere."[14]

During his brief five-day stay, Lummis viewed with keen interest all aspects of life on a New Mexican hacienda. With Amado as his guide, he visited the far-flung cattle and sheep camps and watched vaqueros with smoking irons burn the Chaves CY brand on the left hip of new calves.[15] Lummis also met Cuate, Manuel's devoted *mayordomo*, who bossed the scores of cowboys and shepherds working the stock, and explored several large Indian ruins on a ridge near the main ranch house. One day Amado rode with him to San Miguel camp, a heavily fortified adobe structure Manuel had built near the site where his brother and other Cebolletans had been massacred by Navajos after the campaign of 1851. Here, too, Billy the Kid, before he gained notoriety in the Lincoln County War, had hid out following his killing of Frank Cahill of Camp Grant, Arizona.[16]

Manuel Chaves' brand.

Román A. Baca's brand.

Cuate, mayordomo of the Chaves hacienda at San Mateo, 1888. *Charles Lummis photo.*

Probably more than anything else, the youthful Lummis was impressed by the spacious house presided over by Manuel Chaves and by the tempo of life that pulsed within. Mealtimes the table was bountifully laden with native fare: Indian stews of mutton and hominy, beef roasted in cubes and laced with sauce of red chile, hard cakes called *galletas*, tinned fruits, wine, and coffee. Of the bread Lummis commented, "It was white and graham of home-made flour, not robbed of its nutrition by roller processes, and baked in the big adobe ovens of the courtyard." He declared that "the large scale of housekeeping at such a hacienda may be inferred from the one item of coffee, of which 2,500 pounds was consumed there yearly."[17]

Of the last evening of his idyllic visit, Lummis wrote with feeling:

> We gathered in one of the big rooms, by the rollicking light of the adobe fireplace and sang the sweet Spanish folksong and played happy, simple games. The old hero Don, wasted with disease from many wounds and fifty years of incomparable hardships, his Madonna-faced wife, his very beautiful daughters and dashing sons, and cousins and friends, old and young—how the faces all come back to me, though so many of the dearest sleep under the long shadow of the noble peak of San Mateo.[18]

As Lummis indicated, Manuel during his last years suffered intensely the effects of his hard life. Old wounds in his legs pained and bled, his vision dimmed, and the tough, wiry frame that once weighed 140, now emaciated, was down to less than a hundred pounds.[19] But all was borne stoically, the Little Lion having lived much too long to accept defeat at this late date. Once he was out in a field

Manuel Chaves, 1888. *Charles Lummis photo.*

with his grandson Rodolfo Otero, watching the boy perform some clever shooting with a new Winchester.

"Try it, grandpa," Rodolfo urged the old man. Manuel disliked the modern repeating rifles, his single-shot muzzle loader having rendered long and faithful service. But finally he yielded and took up the new weapon.

"Go put a mark on that cedar," he said, pointing to a twisted tree a hundred yards away. Rodolfo ran over and, considerate of his grandfather's disabilities, fastened a six-inch paper to the trunk.

"Va!" snorted Manuel in disgust. "What do you think, *hijito*, that I'm like a mole. Go back with this bullet and make a mark on the paper."

When Rodolfo had complied, the ancient marksman squinted at the target that fluttered slightly in the breeze and, throwing the rifle to his shoulder, fired instantly. "Now," he said wryly, "it sees itself better." And he shot again with the same rapidity. When they walked up to the tree, the boy observed with awe that the first bullet had taken away his mark, and the second had landed so close that the flattened bits of lead touched. Manuel probably smiled to himself; he'd not lost his old skill.[20]

Educated in the frontier school of harsh experience, Don Manuel firmly believed that strenuous work was the best remedy for his physical afflictions. During the lambing or branding season, he could often be found horseback with his men, doing his feeble best and occasionally taking hard knocks. In 1885 a newspaper story reported briefly one of these very hard knocks. "Hon. Amado Chaves is in the city on a visit and has 300 sheep driven up from his San Mateo ranch for sale here. His father recently met with a very serious accident, a vicious steer having caught him up and tossed him over. The brute's horn tore away the flesh making a wound at least a foot in length, but fortunately the point did not penetrate the abdomen."[21]

In his later days, Manuel was often approached to run for public office, but though a staunch Republican, he eschewed a political life. He was content for Amado and his brother Román to play a significant role in territorial government, both men serving conspicuously in the legislature.[22] The New Mexican militia was something else; until his death, Don Manuel commanded Company F of San Mateo.[23] The position, with Indian troubles all but subsided, was an honorific one. A brief note in a Santa Fe paper in 1883, under the heading "Militia Melange," reminded readers that "Captain Manuel Chaves of the San Mateo Rifles has the reputation of being one of the best Indian fighters in the country. He was a lieutenant-colonel of New Mexican volunteers during the war."[24] A small bit of recognition, but evidence nonetheless that territorial citizens remembered what the Little Lion had done.

When Manuel had first come to San Mateo, he stood in front of his oaks, bent with age, as he was himself, and pondered. Perhaps he saw them as symbolic of his own stubborn hardihood, saw them anchored in the sand and red clay of New Mexico, and making a go of it where others surely would have failed. Though, as we have seen, he was not given to formal religion, he decided, nevertheless, to build a chapel under these spreading branches. The structure which he raised from the earth was small and plain, its floor hard-packed dirt and its spare altar adorned with a few home carved saints. Vicenta was especially pleased to have a place for family worship, and over the succeeding years it was she who led the household there in prayers and an occasional novena. According to tradition, Archbishop Lamy, on one of his Apostolic visits to Tucson, descended from the Santa Fe stage long enough to bless Manuel's chapel.[25] If this actually occurred, it may have represented something of a reconciliation of the earlier feud over fences and boundaries at Guadalupe Chapel.

In late January of 1889 a bulletin went out from Grants Station south of San Mateo. The Little Lion had finally been defeated; the light had flickered out at last.[26] Manuel's casket was a hollowed log prepared by his sons, and he was placed to rest, according to the Spanish custom of his ancestors, beneath the altar of his chapel. When his beloved Vicenta followed him in death six years later, she was laid beside him.[27] And as the spring winds swept off the highest crags of the San Mateo Peaks, the oak leaves whispered:

> He sleeps his last sleep,
> He has fought his last battle;
> No sound can waken him to glory again.

The Manuel Chaves hacienda at San Mateo as it appears today. Presently it serves as the headquarters for the Fernández Cattle Company. The small log building at far right marks the site of Manuel's chapel. The cottonwoods are those planted by his son Irineo. *Author photo.*

Epilogue

Eminent western historian Walter Prescott Webb once wrote, "People love their heroic periods, make legends about them, and vaguely hope they will come again." Manuel Antonio Chaves lived in such a period; he excelled in the arduous and dangerous trade of pioneering, and when his work was done, he left among his people a legend of leonine proportions. As with most builders of the American West around whom a mythic cloud gathered, Manuel's great deeds and accomplishments were enlarged in the telling. Yet, as the facts of this story have demonstrated, from a roisterous boyhood on the frontier to the painful twilight of his years, suffered with monumental dignity, his life was filled with enough adventure, achievement, and service to burnish the shields of several men.

Too few of our Spanish frontiersmen have been studied in depth. They had to face the same or similar problems encountered by Anglo-American settlers, but their responses and solutions often differed significantly. For example,

Manuel Chaves, in spite of decades of hardship and heartache imposed by his conflict with the Indians, never became an "Indian hater." Nor did any New Mexican, at least in the sense the term applied to so many of the men who ventured west of the Mississippi. The Spanish people fought the Indians when they felt the occasion demanded it, but in times of peace they were quick to forget past grievances, accepting their old losses with philosophical resignation and mingling amiably with warriors whom they had opposed yesterday and might fight again tomorrow. In retrospect, we see that their struggles with the Indians were tempered by the realization that they fought against a worthy foe, their long view tinged with no prejudice against race. Until this is clearly understood, the life and work of a man like Manuel Chaves cannot be seen in proper perspective.

Manuel, his kin, his times are now gone with the winds of vanished years. No more do men ride great distances muleback across our southwestern deserts or unlimber their weapons when they see an Indian in the hills or build a thousand piñon campfires in the course of their lives. Rugged courage, self-sufficiency, skill at arms, and physical endurance no longer command the premium they once did. And men such as Manuel Antonio Chaves, whom Lummis described as "a courtly Spanish gentleman, brave as a lion, tender as a woman, spotless of honor, and modest as heroic," are rare indeed.

Notes

Introduction

1. The Amado Chaves Collection cited below represents material assembled at a later date.
2. Charles F. Lummis, *Mesa, Cañon and Pueblo,* viii.

Chapter 1: Roots

1. The original and correct spelling of the family name was Chaves, but in New Mexico only Manuel Antonio's direct descendants retained this form, other lines changing the final "s" to "z."
2. Eleanor B. Adams (ed.), *Tamaron's Visitation of New Mexico, 1760,* 44.
3. This date of Manuel's birth is given by his son Amado in a manuscript found in the "Manuel Antonio Chaves File," History Library, Museum of New Mexico, Santa Fe (cited hereinafter as Chaves Ms., Mus. of N.M.). This date was followed in the biographical sketch of Manuel presented by Ralph Emerson Twitchell in his *History of the Military*

Occupation of New Mexico, 292; and by Charles F. Lummis in *A New Mexico David,* 193. Nevertheless, the foremost historian of the Chaves family, Fray Angélico Chávez notes in his *Origins of New Mexico Families,* 324, that Manuel's early records, including his baptismal certificate, are not extant, and that the usually accepted birth date is probably incorrect. This would seem to be borne out by two documents of a later period. The first, a militia muster roll of January 23, 1847 (Adjutant General Muster Rolls, No. 18, State Records Center and Archives, Santa Fe), gives his age as twenty-six, indicating he was born in 1820, perhaps on October 18 of that year. The second document, also a muster roll and dated November 25, 1862 (Field and Staff Muster Roll, "Compiled Service Record for Manuel Antonio Chaves, 1861-1863," Records of the War Department, National Archives, Washington, D.C.), lists the age of Manuel Chaves as forty-two years, placing his birth again in 1820.

4. The town of Chaves was founded by the Romans in A.D. 74, the location apparently being selected because of the presence of thermal springs. An impressive stone bridge was constructed across the Rio Tamega which lasted until early in the twentieth century. The town was first taken by the Moors in 716, and in succeeding centuries passed, on various occasions, between them and the Spaniards. See *Enciclopedia Universal Ilustrada,* Vol. XVII, 120-21; and Genealogical Notes, Amado Chaves Collection, State Records Center and Archives, Santa Fe (cited hereinafter as A. Chaves Col., St. Rec. Cen.).
5. Twitchell, *Military Occupation,* 287-88; Anonymous, "The Name of Chaves," *El Palacio,* 22 (1927), 112-16; *Enciclopedia Heráldica y Genealógica Hispano Americana,* XXVIII, 54-66. Historian Ralph E. Twitchell obtained much information on Chaves family history directly from the Duke of La Semana who was employed at the royal court in Madrid. Cf. Amado Chaves to Brian Boru Dunn, Cowles, New Mexico, June 18, 1924, in A. Chaves Col., St. Rec. Cen.
6. Chávez, *Origins of New Mexico Families,* 19, 23.
7. Anonymous, "The Name of Chaves," 115-16; and Lansing

B. Bloom, "Necrology, Amado Chaves," *New Mexico Historical Review*, 6 (1931), 101-104.

8. Chávez, *Origins of New Mexico Families*, 19. The source for the statement that the New Mexico Chaveses were descended from Ruí López (de Chaves) is a letter from Harry H. Hallah, U.S. Vice Consul in Madrid to Amado Chaves, March 9, 1903 (A. Chaves Col., St. Rec. Cen.). Hallah assembled historical material pertaining to the Chaves name from the Count of Caudilla, who was head of the family in Spain, and sent it on to Amado in New Mexico (Hallah to Chaves, Madrid, April 29, 1903, ibid.). At the same time a watercolor facsimile of the Chaves coat-of-arms, showing the five keys on a center shield, was prepared under direction of the Count. This representation is now in the possession of Mrs. Consuelo Chaves Summers of Santa Fe.
9. Chávez, *Origins of New Mexico Families*, 23; Fray Angélico Chávez, "Don Fernando Durán de Chávez," *El Palacio*, 55 (1948), 105-07.
10. Ibid., 114.
11. Chávez, *Origins of New Mexico Families*, 33, 181.
12. The principal sources for the story of the Tomé massacre are two: Lummis, *A New Mexico David*, 94-100; and Allen A. Carter, "The Legend of Tomé," an unpublished manuscript in the files of the New Mexico Writers' project, Santa Fe. Other records which help confirm various details are: Records of Burial in Tomé, May 26, 1777 (of twenty men killed by Comanches), Archives of the Archdiocese of Santa Fe, Albuquerque, Books of Burials, no. 3; and Certificate of the Burial of the Victims of the Tomé Massacre, Fray Andrés García, 1777, cited by Adolph Bandelier, *Report of the United States Commission to the Columbian Historical Exposition at Madrid, 1892-1893*, 317.
13. Lummis, *A New Mexico David*, 100.
14. Statement on Chaves Genealogy entitled "Questions" in A. Chaves Col., St. Rec. Cen.
15. Chávez, *Origins of New Mexico Families*, 324.
16. Gilberto Espinosa and Tibo J. Chaves, *El Rio Abajo*, 191.
17. Ruth Laughlin Barker, *Caballeros*, 55.

Chapter 2: Youth

1. J.M. Pearce (ed.), *New Mexico Place Names, A Geographical Dictionary,* 29. The modern spelling of the town name is Seboyeta.
2. Information on the early history of Cebolleta can be found in official documents numbered 1754, 1758, and 1763 from the Spanish Archives of New Mexico, State Records Center and Archives, Santa Fe. Charles Lummis recorded the deeds of Señora Romero and Domingo Baca in his volume *A New Mexico David,* 195-96. He secured his facts from interviews with Cebolletans during the late nineteenth century.
3. Chávez, *Origins of New Mexico Families,* 324.
4. Details on Román's parentage and birth are taken from an undated news clipping (ca. 1899) titled "Death of Román A. Baca" in the Prince Collection, State Records Center and Archives, Santa Fe.
5. Ralph Emerson Twitchell, *The Leading Facts of New Mexican History,* II, 304.
6. Amado Chaves to Laurence F. Lee, Santa Fe, September 23, 1927 (A. Chaves Col., St. Rec. Cen.). The price of $500 for an Indian captive perhaps seems excessive, but the identical figure appears often in contemporary accounts. Since currency was scarce and barter widespread, most slaves were doubtless paid for in goods or livestock.
7. Lummis, *A New Mexico David,* 198.
8. Chaves Ms., Mus. of N.M.; and Twitchell, *Military Occupation of New Mexico,* 293. It should be noted that historian Twitchell in writing of Manuel relied heavily on information supplied by Amado, although it may be presumed that he was able to verify certain details when he personally interviewed the old campaigner in the late 1880s.
9. Although most sources fix Canyon de Chelly as the site, Lummis suggests it was the Canyon de Chusca further north. "A New Mexican Hero," *St. Louis Daily Globe-Democrat,* August 15, 1888. This article and a similar one, "A New Mexico Hero," in the *Daily New Mexican,* Santa Fe, March 25, 1891, complement and in some particulars expand upon Lummis' sketch of Manuel Chaves in his *A New Mexico*

David. 190-217. It should perhaps be noted that Manuel Chaves is *not* the "David" of Lummis' book, the subtitle of which accurately describes the various chapters: "And Other Stories and Sketches of the Southwest." The title chapter, "A New Mexico David," is the account of an expedition against the Utes led by Manuel Chaves, but the hero—the David—of the story is Lucario Montoya. The chapter devoted to Manuel Chaves is entitled "A New Mexican Hero."

10. Amado Chaves wrote to Ralph E. Twitchell: "*Carnaza* was what the Indian [Pahe] used to stuff his wound. I do not know the English name. It is that light stuff inside of buckskin. You can remove it with your finger and apply it to a wound and the bleeding will stop at once." (Letter, February 11, 1909, Chaves File, Mus. of N.M.)
11. The sole source for this incident is Lummis, "A New Mexican Hero," *St. Louis Daily Globe-Democrat,* August 5, 1888.

Chapter 3: The Fugitive

1. Lummis, "A New Mexican Hero," *St. Louis Daily Globe-Democrat,* August 5, 1888. In other particulars Lummis demonstrates that he may have confused the New Orleans trip with a later journey Manuel made to the United States.
2. My inclusion of Manuel in Armijo's army is based upon inference derived from Amado Chaves' statement that his father first came to Santa Fe in 1837 (Chaves Ms., Mus. of N.M.). This supposition is further supported by Manuel's close association at this time with his uncle Mariano, who played a conspicuous role in the events of 1837, and by the fact that Manuel soon received a commission in the militia.
3. Professor Daniel Tyler, in a letter to the author, fixes the date of Armijo's birth as 1792 (Personal correspondence, November 10, 1970). See also Daniel Tyler, "Gringo Views of Manuel Armijo," *New Mexico Historical Review,* 45 (1970), 23-46.
4. Lansing Bartlett Bloom, "New Mexico Under Mexican Administration, 1822-1846," *Old Santa Fe,* 1 (January, 1914), 266.

5. Ibid., 2 (July, 1914), 25-26.
6. Chávez, *Origins of New Mexico Families*, 323.
7. Twitchell, *Leading Facts of New Mexican History*, II, 25.
8. Stella M. Drumm (ed.), *Down the Santa Fe Trail and Into Mexico: The Diary of Susan Shelby Magoffin, 1846-1847*, 154.
9. W.H.H. Allison, quoting from the recollections of Colonel Francisco Perea, "Santa Fe As It Appeared During the Winter of the Years 1837 and 1838," *Old Santa Fe*, 2 (October, 1914), 172.
10. Although Mariano Chávez is here referred to as Manuel's uncle, he was certainly more distantly related than this term implies. Mariano was definitely not the brother of Julián Chaves, Manuel's father. Since most of the older generation New Mexicans were related to each other in several ways, their use of kinship terms was somewhat arbitrary, being based more upon convenience or familiarity of association. For example, close companions even today address each other as *primo,* cousin, whether this is their actual blood relationship or not. Thus, if Manuel was attached to Mariano's household for several years, as seems the case, his occasional reference to him as *tio,* uncle, would have been natural.
11. Considerable discrepancy exists in details surrounding the events of 1837-1838. Most writers have relied heavily on tradition and second-hand accounts, giving little attention to documentary evidence. The full story must await that scholar who will mine the voluminous resources available in the Mexican Archives of New Mexico, Santa Fe. In the meanwhile, two recent articles offer new insights into the affair: Fray Angélico Chávez, "José Gonzalez, Genízaro Governor," *New Mexico Historical Review,* 30 (1955), 190-94; and Phillip Reno, "Rebellion in New Mexico — 1837," *NMHR*, 40 (1965), 197-213.
12. Bloom, "New Mexico Under Mexican Administration," *Old Santa Fe,* 1 (January, 1914), 134n.
13. Armijo's mother, Doña Barbara Chaves, was a sister of Manuel's father, Julián, so actually Manuel and the governor were cousins (Ralph Emerson Twitchell, *Old Santa Fe*, 338n). However, because of the difference in their ages,

young Manuel customarily addressed Armijo as uncle, while the governor referred to him as his nephew Manuelito. This has led some writers to assume Armijo and Chaves were really uncle and nephew. Actually the genealogies of the leading families were so interwoven that this relationship may have also prevailed. See note 10 above. Lummis occasionally refers to Armijo as Manuel's great-uncle.

14. Amado Chaves says the amount of the bet was $5,000 (Letter to R.E. Twitchell, Albuquerque, February 20, 1909, Chaves File, Mus. of N.M., hereinafter cited as A. Chaves to Twitchell, 1909), while Lummis gives the sum as $7,000 ("A New Mexican Hero," *St. Louis Daily Globe-Democrat,* August 5, 1888). These are the two principal sources for this incident.
15. Typed statement of Amado Chaves, Misc. Papers, A. Chaves Col., St. Rec. Cen.; and Fray Angélico Chávez, "Doña Tules, Her Fame and Her Funeral," *El Palacio,* 57 (1950), 229.
16. A description of the card game monte can be found in Walter Briggs, "The Lady They Called Tules," *New Mexico Magazine,* 49 (1971), 9-16.
17. Drumm, *Down the Santa Fe Trail,* 53n.
18. A short biographical sketch of P.A. Masure appears in Drumm, *Down the Santa Fe Trail,* 53n. Also personal correspondence, David J. Weber to Marc Simmons, San Diego, December 13, 1968. Twitchell refers to "an old French doctor living with Scolly" (239) and provides a brief description of John Scolly, known to the Mexicans as Juan Escólle (*Old Santa Fe,* 236n).
19. Again, as in note 14 above, there is a discrepancy in the figures provided by the two principal accounts. Lummis says Armijo offered the doctor $1,000; Amado Chaves gives $1,500. Since Lummis presumably took notes when he interviewed Manuel Chaves, while Amado wrote years later from memory, the former's word has been relied upon in this instance.
20. Twitchell says that "Colonel Manuel Chaves told the writer that he considered General Armijo a great coward; that he knew him only too well; that at one time he laid in wait for him to come out of the palace intending to kill him

with an arrow." (*Leading Facts of New Mexican History*, II, 67n) Twitchell also claims that Chaves repeated to him the familiar statement often attributed to Armijo: "It is better to be thought brave than to really be so."

21. The doctor returned to New Mexico in 1846 in the wake of General Stephen W. Kearny's conquering army. On the trail he often attended young Susan Shelby Magoffin, ailing wife of a prominent trader, who described him in her diary as "an excellent physician, especially in female cases." (Drumm, *Down the Santa Fe Trail*, 53)
22. The principal sources for Manuel's activities in St. Louis are A. Chaves to Twitchell, 1909; and two pieces by Lummis previously cited, "A New Mexican Hero," *St. Louis Daily Globe-Democrat*, August 5, 1888; and *A New Mexico David*, 201. Where accounts of the authors differ, I have generally, though not invariably, accepted the version of Amado Chaves. One instance of this concerns Manuel's pursuit of Fernández. Lummis claims Manuel abandoned the chase in New York for lack of funds, whereas Amado says his father continued to Cuba. Attempts to locate other sources which might add to or clarify the Amado Chaves and Lummis narratives have proved futile. For example, a search of the Archives of the Missouri Historical Society revealed nothing on Manuel Chaves, Navarro, or Alfonso Fernández (Frances H. Stadler, Archivist, to Marc Simmons, St. Louis, February 21, 1969). Lummis gives the name of Manuel's benefactor as Navarrez rather than Navarro. This might be a corruption of Navalles. According to the *St. Louis Directory for the Years 1838-39* by Charles Keemle, a J. Navalles operated a grocery business and coffee house on Second Street, between Mulberry and Lombard (William A. Goff to Marc Simmons, Kansas City, Mo., May 18, 1969).
23. Max L. Moorhead, *New Mexico's Royal Road*, 195; and Ward Alan Minge, "Frontier Problems in New Mexico Preceding the Mexican War, 1840-1846," 247.
24. A. Chaves to Twitchell, 1909.
25. Ibid.

Chapter 4: Santa Fe

1. Dorman H. Winfrey, "Mirabeau B. Lamar and Texas Nationalism," *Southwestern Historical Quarterly,* 59 (1955), 186.
2. Charles Adams Gulick, Jr., *et al.* (eds.), *The Papers of Mirabeau Buonaparte Lamar,* II, 368.
3. Ibid., III, 370-71.
4. Winfrey, "Lamar and Texas Nationalism," 191.
5. Quoted by George Wilkins Kendall in his *Narrative of the Texan Santa Fe Expedition,* as cited by Twitchell, *Old Santa Fe,* 204n. Kendall, a reporter for the *New Orleans Daily Picayune,* had accompanied the expedition as an observer, and his book, which first appeared in 1844, became the classic account of the episode.
6. F.W. Hodge (ed.), "Combs Narrative of the Santa Fe Expedition in 1841," *New Mexico Historical Review,* 5 (1930), 308. Prior to 1845, when Texas became the twenty-eighth state, Texans were called Texians.
7. Ibid.
8. The role Manuel Chaves played in the capture of the Texans has been missed by virtually every writer on the subject. Combs speaks only of the governor's nephew and secretary, without naming him. Thomas Falconer, another participant, in his *Letters and Notes on the Texan Santa Fe Expedition, 1841-1842,* 53, refers to Captain Lewis' companion as Don M. Chaves. Unfortunately, this led most authors to assume the man was Mariano Chávez, an impossibility since he was certainly not Armijo's nephew. Thus William Binkley in his article, "New Mexico and the Texan-Santa Fe Expedition," *Southwestern Historical Quarterly,* 28 (1923), 102-03, makes the statement, "Mariano Chaves was ordered to be ready to take command of part of the troops on short notice." Assuming the original source was intended to mean Manuel Chaves, I assign him the command of reinforcements which joined Captain Salazar near Anton Chico.

   Further confusion is created by Josiah Gregg who treated the matter briefly in his *Commerce of the Prairies.* Although writing not long after the event, Gregg depended upon sources of dubious reliability. He says, "It is asserted that Mariano Chávez furnished a considerable quantity of provisions, blankets, etc. to Col. Cooke's division of Texan prisoners." (341) Again, I ascribe this act to Manuel rather than Mariano. Almost inexplicable is a further note by Gregg which declares, "The family of Mariano Chávez is very distinct from one Manuel Chaves (who, though Gov. Armijo's nephew, is a very low character), a principal agent in the treacheries practised on the Texan Santa Fe expedition." The only part of this statement containing a germ of truth is the reference to Manuel as Armijo's nephew. For the rest, I attribute it to misinformation collected by Gregg. Actually, another nephew of Armijo's, Tomás Martínez, led an attack on the house of the American consul in Santa Fe during the governor's absence and thereby earned an unsavory reputation. Perhaps some of Gregg's befuddlement can be traced to a confusion of nephews. In any event, there is ample evidence concerning the honorable part played by Manuel Chaves in this affair, while I can find no unquestionable source to prove the participation of Mariano, although it is not unlikely that he was a member of Armijo's staff.

The clincher would seem to be provided by writings of Amado Chaves, especially his Chaves Ms., and Lummis' *A New Mexico David*, 202, which, though much garbled in detail, definitely attribute a significant role in the capture of the Texans to Manuel Chaves.

9. Some accounts say this was done under Salazar's direction, but owing to the subsequent barbarous treatment accorded the prisoners by this man, those sources that seem to link Manuel Chaves with the distribution of provisions appear more acceptable.
10. Hodge, "Combs' Narrative," 309.
11. Ibid., 310.
12. Chaves Ms., Mus. of N.M.
13. W.H.H. Allison (ed.), "Santa Fe As It Appeared During the Winter of the Years 1837 and 1838," *Old Santa Fe*, 2 (1914), 178. The description of Manuel's house by Colonel

Perea was supposed to have been for the period 1837-1838, but since his reminiscence was set down some fifty years after the fact, I believe the Colonel erred, and the house he remembered actually dated from the early 1840s, following Manuel's return from St. Louis.

14. Chaves Ms., Mus. of N.M.
15. *Death Comes for the Archbishop,* 184. Cather's references to Manuel Chaves in this historical novel were based upon interviews with Amado. See Mary Austin, *Earth Horizon, An Autobiography,* 359.
16. *Santa Fe New Mexican,* March 21, 1899.
17. Wayne L. Mauzy, "Recollections of Demetrio Pérez: The Old Palace in Mexican Day," *El Palacio,* 67 (1967), 92. In A. Chaves to Twitchell, 1909, Amado says, "My father raised Don Román from the time he was nine years old."
18. According to Chávez, *Origins of New Mexico Families,* 325, María Vicenta was born on October 29, 1829 at Tomé.
19. Ibid., 223.
20. Ibid., 202.
21. Misc. Notes, A. Chaves Col., St. Rec. Cen.; and Ralph E. Twitchell, *The Spanish Archives of New Mexico,* I, 198.
22. Sketch of Doña Tules, A. Chaves Col., St. Rec. Cen.; and Twitchell, *Spanish Archives,* I, 198-99.
23. These portraits, reproduced in this volume, are now in the possession of Manuel's great-grandson, Amado Chaves Summers of Santa Fe.
24. Willa Cather, *Death Comes for the Archbishop,* 183.
25. Fr. Angélico Chávez to Marc Simmons, Peña Blanca, New Mexico, January 4, 1970.
26. LeRoy R. Hafen (ed.), *Ruxton of the Rockies,* 176.
27. W.H.H. Allison (ed.), "Santa Fe in 1846," *Old Santa Fe,* 2 (1915), 395; and Mauzy, "Recollections of Demetrio Pérez," 92.
28. Minge, "Frontier Problems in New Mexico," 262.
29. Ibid., 263.
30. Ibid., 264.
31. There are numerous accounts of the Ute affair, all of them varying in minor details. See e.g., Mauzy, "Recollections of Demetrio Pérez," 92-93; Benjamin Read, *Illustrated History*

of New Mexico, 410-11; and the version related in the *Santa Fe New Mexican,* October 31, 1891.

Chapter 5: Fortunes of War

1. Quoted in Frederick Merk, *Manifest Destiny and Mission in American History,* 110.
2. Quoted in Howard Roberts Lamar, *The Far Southwest, 1846-1912,* 57.
3. Quoted in Bernard DeVoto, *The Year of Decision, 1846,* 251-52.
4. Lansing B. Bloom, "New Mexico Under Mexican Administration," *Old Santa Fe,* 2 (1915), 363. Mariano Barela's report is contained in José M. Ponce de León (ed.), *Reseñas Históricas del Estado de Chihuahua,* 337-38.
5. Ibid., 369.
6. The incident surrounding Armijo's abandonment of his position and subsequent flight to Mexico has been described in numerous accounts. See e.g., George Rutledge Gibson, *Journal of a Soldier Under Kearny and Doniphan, 1846-1847,* 73, 81, 88; and Ross Calvin (ed.), *Lieutenant Emory Reports,* in which the statement appears, "It is well known that he [Armijo] has been averse to a battle, but some of his people threatened his life if he refused to fight." (53) Chaves' presence at Apache Pass as a militia officer is confirmed by Amado in Chaves Ms., Mus. of N.M.
7. George Winston Smith and Charles Judah (eds.), "Manifest Destiny: War in the West," *New Mexico Quarterly,* 38 (1968), 47.
8. James Madison Cutts, *The Conquest of California and New Mexico,* 221.
9. The full list of those who initiated plans to overthrow the American regime was given in later years to historian Ralph E. Twitchell by Colonel Manuel Chaves, Captain Román A. Baca, and Don Nicolás Pino; see Twitchell, *Old Santa Fe,* 276n.
10. W.W.H. Davis, *El Gringo, Or New Mexico & Her People* 296-97.

11. Briggs, "La Tules," 9-16.
12. Twitchell, *Military Occupation*, 298-99.
13. Quoted in ibid., 299; and Chaves Ms., Mus. of N.M.
14. A. Chaves to Twitchell, 1909.
15. After being mustered out of service in Missouri at the conclusion of the war, William Angney returned to New Mexico; he practiced law and became active in territorial politics.
16. Twitchell, *Military Occupation*, 300; and Chaves Ms., Mus. of N.M.
17. Lamar, *The Far Southwest*, 68.
18. *Dictionary of American Biography*, I, 305-06.
19. David Lavender, *Bent's Fort*, 290.
20. Twitchell, *Military Occupation*, 300.
21. Adjutant General Muster Rolls, No. 18 (St. Vrain Company, 1847), New Mexico State Records Center and Archives, Santa Fe.
22. Price's report is printed in Cutts, *The Conquest of California and New Mexico*, 223-31.
23. Ibid., 229.
24. Descriptions of the Battle of Taos are contained in John T. Hughes, *Doniphan's Expedition*, 394-96; and E. Bennett Burton, "The Taos Rebellion," *Old Santa Fe*, 1 (1913), 176-209.
25. Chaves Ms., Mus. of N.M.; Lummis, *A New Mexico David*, 205. A well-known frontiersman, "Uncle Dick" Wootton later claimed the honor of rescuing St. Vrain at the Taos battle; see Howard Louis Conrad, *"Uncle Dick" Wootton*, 364. However, a report in the *Weekly New Mexico Review*, August 16, 1894, confirms that Manuel Chaves was responsible for the feat. It asserts that St. Vrain in gratitude offered to share with Manuel part of his several-million-acre Animas Land Grant in southeastern Colorado.

Chapter 6: An Interlude

1. Genealogical Notes, A. Chaves Col., St. Rec. Cen.
2. Deed Book A (Registro), Santa Fe County Records, 334-37.
3. "Necrology, Amado Chaves," *New Mexico Historical Review*, 6 (1931), 100; and Amado Chaves to R.E. Twitchell, Santa

Fe, October 19, 1922, Chaves File, Mus. of N.M. Amado's full name was José Anacleto Amado de Jesus Chaves. In later years he wrote: "When Beatriz Labadie, the daughter of my uncle Don Lorenzo Labadie, was born, I was five years old. My aunt Rallitos had the baby baptized eight days after her birth. The little girl was beautifully dressed, and when the party returned from the church, my aunt placed her in the lap of my mother saying, '*Hermanita, hay te la novia de Amado.* Sister, there you have Amado's bride.' My mother said, 'I accept her with all my heart.' As we grew up we considered ourselves engaged, and if I had not gone to Washington to be educated, we surely would have got married." (Amado Chaves to Laurence Lee, Albuquerque, September 23, 1927, A. Chaves Col., St. Rec. Cen.)

4. The partnership is referred to in Lorenzo's obituary that appeared in the *Santa Fe New Mexican,* August 11, 1904.
5. Annie Heloise Abel (ed.), "The Journal of John Griener," *Old Santa Fe,* 3 (1916), 210.
6. Amado Chaves to Laurence Lee, Albuquerque, September 23, 1927, A. Chaves Col., St. Rec. Cen.
7. Abel, "Journal of John Griener," 210.
8. Manuel Chaves to Felipe Chaves, Santa Fe, July 2, 1852, Felipe Chaves Papers, St. Rec. Cen. In this letter Manuel alludes briefly to a trip to California, but gives no details. It is a fair guess that he went in company with other New Mexicans driving sheep to the booming markets in the gold camps.
9. Amado refers to Armenta in his letter to R.E. Twitchell, Santa Fe, October 19, 1922, Chaves File, Mus. of N.M., and mentions that the servant once lived in the ancient adobe building near San Miguel Chapel that is today referred to as the oldest house in the United States.
10. Deed Book A (Registro), Santa Fe County Records, 335-37.
11. Josiah Gregg, *Commerce of the Prairies,* 175. Regarding medals of Nuestra Señora de Guadalupe, Gregg remarks, "I have been informed 216,000 were struck at Birmingham in the year 1831, designed for the Mexican market." Manuel's medal is now in the A. Chaves Col., St. Rec. Cen.
12. Personal interview with Consuelo Chaves Summers, Santa

Fe, Oct. 22, 1968. Mrs. Summers told this writer that she heard her father, Amado Chaves, relate the details of this incident on several occasions. The matter is also referred to briefly in an untitled summary history of the Chaves family in the A. Chaves Col., St. Rec. Cen.

Chapter 7: The Indian Fighter

1. Annie Heloise Abel (ed.), *The Official Correspondence of James S. Calhoun*, 283.
2. Ramon Luna's official report of the expedition appears in ibid., 284-86. Accounts of the massacre in San Miguel Canyon can be found in Lummis, *A New Mexico David*, 196-98; and C.C. Marino, "The Seboyetans and the Navajos," *New Mexico Historical Review*, 29 (1954), 23-25. Lummis declares that the body of Pedro Chaves was decapitated and his head carried to the summit of San Mateo Peak.
3. John S. Watts, *Indian Depredations in New Mexico*, 29.
4. Ibid., 5.
5. Abel, *Official Correspondence*, 500-01.
6. Ibid, 302-03. Manuel's proposals were written in Spanish and "a literal translation of the original" was provided by D.V. Whiting. According to Amado, Manuel spoke fair English as a result of his early stay in St. Louis, but his letters written in this language indicate he was quite fluent.
7. Ibid., 301.
8. Records of the Office of Indian Affairs, Vol. 47, Jan. 21-Aug. 24, 1853, Reel 47 of Microfilms, University of New Mexico, Special Collections, Albuquerque. Carson, like other Indian agents, was required to post a $5,000 bond and received an annual salary of $1,500.
9. Report of Kit Carson, Taos Agency, March 21, 1854. Bureau of Indian Affairs, Superintendency of New Mexico, 1849-1880, Reel 1 of Microfilms, University of New Mexico, Special Collections, Albuquerque.
10. Morris F. Taylor, "Campaigns Against the Jicarilla Apache, 1855," *New Mexico Historical Review*, 45 (1970), 121.
11. Misc. Militia Records and Muster Rolls, 1855, Adjutant

General's Files, New Mexico State Records Center and Archives.

12. Chris Emmett, *Fort Union and the Winning of the Southwest,* 188.
13. Edwin L. Sabin, *Kit Carson Days,* II, 667.
14. Ibid., 668. According to a popular story, the scalping knife wielded by Tapia later came into the possession of Major Richard Weightman who used it when he stabbed to death long-distance rider F.X. Aubry in a Santa Fe brawl. This was patently impossible, however, since Aubry was slain the summer prior to the Ute-Jicarilla campaign.
15. Quoted in Blanche C. Grant, *When Old Trails Were New, The Story of Taos,* 311.
16. Morris F. Taylor, "Action at Fort Massachusetts: The Indian Campaign of 1855," *Colorado Magazine,* 42 (1965), 304-07.
17. This letter was printed in the *Santa Fe New Mexican,* January 23, 1893, after the original had come into the possession of then Governor L. Bradford Prince. It also appears in Twitchell, *Military Occupation,* 302-03.
18. Taylor, "Campaign Against the Jicarilla," 129-30.
19. *Santa Fe Weekly Gazette,* October 31, 1857.
20. Twitchell, *Military Occupation,* 304. Although no specific record of Manuel's salary has been found, I have assumed here that it was the same as assigned to Blas Lucero, chief scout and packer for the southern wing of the Expedition. See Emmett, *Fort Union,* 205.
21. This speech was recorded by Amado in his Chaves Ms., Mus. of N.M.
22. Ibid.
23. Twitchell, *Military Occupation,* 304-05.
24. The canyon where Cuchillo Negro's camp was routed is sometimes mentioned as that of San Vicente and other times as Cañon de los Muertos Carneros in the valley of the Safo River. None of these place names can be identified with certainty, but the location of the battle was likely at what is now Cuchillo Arroyo in south central New Mexico.
25. An account of Manuel Chaves' part in this expedition, containing many inaccuracies, is given in Lummis, *A New Mexico David,* 205-207. For example, the author confuses a

more famous Apache chief, Mangas Coloradas, with the slain Cuchillo Negro. He also claims Manuel Chaves led the expedition "clear into the Sierra Madre of Mexico," a statement supported by no other contemporary record. But his assertion that Manuel was cited by the War Department for exceptional services rendered in this campaign is probably true.

26. *Santa Fe Weekly Gazette*, October 31, 1857.
27. Ibid.
28. W.W. Loring, *A Confederate Soldier in Egypt;* and Twitchell, *Military Occupation*, 308.
29. Samuel Woodworth Cozzens, *The Marvellous Country*, 239-51.

Chapter 8: Hacienda de Ojuelos

1. These ruins were excavated in 1969 by archeologists from the University of New Mexico with the permission and cooperation of the Horizon Land Company, present owner of the Tomé Land Grant.
2. Modern topographic maps show one of the higher mountains immediately above Ojuelos as Chaves Peak, perhaps indirect confirmation that Manuel was the first permanent settler in the area. Lorenzo Labadie was still Manuel's partner in the sheep business, but his job with the Indian Service kept him away from Ojuelos much of the time.
3. Personal interview with Boleslo Romero, age fifty-six, of Tomé, September 11, 1970. José Márquez died in 1948 in his late eighties. Quite possibly he was related to Manuel, who is known to have had several cousins named Márquez. Romero admitted to this writer that in the old days everyone in the Tomé district was familiar with the exploits of Manuel Chaves, although at present his name is almost forgotten. As a boy, Romero herded sheep around the ruins of the Ojuelos hacienda.
4. Interview with Consuelo Chaves Summers, Santa Fe, October 22, 1968. Irineo suffered the rest of his life from the effects of this blow to the head. Manuel later sent him to doctors in St. Louis, but they could offer him little relief.

5. Concepción Baca later served as an interpreter for the Apaches with Geronimo who were imprisoned in Florida.
6. Manuel's two brushes with the Apaches are described in Lummis, *A New Mexico David,* 210-14. At the Salada fight, the author states that Vicenta's step-father was also present, but fails to name him.
7. Quoted in William A. Keleher, *Turmoil in New Mexico, 1846-1868,* 103.
8. A.B. Bender, "Frontier Defense in New Mexico, 1853-1861," *New Mexico Historical Review,* 9 (1934), 371.
9. Bender's statement that Cotton probably led the expedition is not true (Ibid., 372). He also says that some Pueblo Indians took part in the venture and brought back 5,000 sheep and horses as their part of the spoils. This probably happened, since the Pueblos had long been accustomed to accompanying the Spaniards in attacks upon the Navajo. No Pueblo Indians, however, were listed in the formal muster rolls. Bender also holds that the expedition was unauthorized, but this clearly was not the case, as indicated by the official records and Cotton's review. Also an entry in Civil War Muster Roll, Descriptive Book, St. Rec. Cen., declares that the men were called out by the authority of the governor.
10. This incident is related by Lummis in *A New Mexico David,* 207-08. Details of the expedition were derived from Adjutant General Records, Militia Descriptive Book (1860), St. Rec. Cen.
11. Frank D. Reeve, "The Federal Indian Policy in New Mexico, 1858-1880," *New Mexico Historical Review,* 12 (1937), 243.
12. Twitchell, *Leading Facts,* II, 319-20.
13. Lummis, *A New Mexico David,* 208-209. Full details of Canby's action against the Navajo can be found in Max L. Heyman, Jr., "On the Navajo Trail: The Campaign of 1860-61," *New Mexico Historical Review,* 26 (1951), 44-63.
14. Manuel was formally mustered into the service of the United States and took the oath of allegiance at Albuquerque, August 1, 1861; on the following day, he was provided an escort of one sergeant, one corporal, and eight privates for the trip to his new command at Fort Fauntleroy (Special Order No. 54, Oath of Manuel Chaves, and Field and Staff Muster Rolls, all in compiled Service Record of Manuel

Chaves, Record Group 94, National Archives, Washington, D.C. Cited hereinafter as R.G. 94, Nat. Arch.).

15. When Colonel Fauntleroy resigned to join the Confederacy, the post was renamed Fort Lyon, but during the Civil War it continued to be referred to as Fort Fauntleroy by many persons. Abandoned for several years, it was reestablished in 1868 and designated as Fort Wingate. Robert W. Frazer, *Forts of the West,* 108.
16. Lt. A.L. Anderson to Col. Manuel Chaves, Santa Fe (Record Group 98, Dept. of New Mexico, Letters Received, 1861, National Archives, Washington, D.C. Cited hereinafter as R.G. 98, Nat. Arch.).
17. "Necrology, Amado Chaves," *New Mexico Historical Review,* 6 (1931), 103-104.
18. Accounts of the horse race are as follows: Report of Manuel Chaves to E.R.S. Canby, September 13, 1861 (R.G. 98, Nat. Arch.); Testimony of Manuel Chaves in his Compiled Service Record (R.G. 94, Nat. Arch.); "A Horse Race in New Mexico in 1861," Ms. in Amado Chaves Collection, St. Rec. Cen.; and Report of Nicholas Hodt, September 7, 1865, from *Condition of the Indian Tribes.* I told the story in my article "Horse Race at Fort Fauntleroy, An Incident of the Navajo Wars," *La Gaceta* of the Santa Fe Corral of the Westerners, 5 (1970), 3-13, but since that writing I have revised several of my conclusions.
19. Very little is known of the personal history of Dr. Kavenaugh. Evidently he came to New Mexico from one of the southern states and resided for many years in Taos. He served as surgeon in St. Vrain's regiment of Mounted Volunteers during the Ute-Jicarilla troubles of 1855, when he first met Manuel Chaves. After New Mexico became involved in the Civil War, the doctor sided with the pro-Southern element in the territory, for which act all his personal property was confiscated by the government at the conclusion of hostilities. As sutler at Fort Fauntleroy, Kavenaugh sold goods at a highly inflated price, occasioning complaint by some persons obliged to do business with him.
20. Canby to Chaves, September 1861, Santa Fe (R.G. 98, Nat. Arch.).
21. Chaves to Canby (Ibid.).

22. Canby to Carson, December 1861 (Ibid.).
23. Compiled Service Record of Manuel Chaves (R.G. 94, Nat. Arch.).
24. Undated petition (Ibid.).
25. Canby to Carson, Belen (Ibid.). The matter of the horse race at Fort Fauntleroy was still a matter of official concern in 1865, when the statement of Captain Nicholas Hodt, cited in note 18 above, was taken. A Congressional Committee on Indian Affairs again looked into the matter, but the record of its conclusions has not been found.

Chapter 9: The Blue and the Gray on the Rio Grande

1. Useful accounts of the Civil War in New Mexico are contained in Robert Lee Kirby, *The Confederate Invasion of Arizona and New Mexico, 1861-1862;* Martin Hardwick Hall, *Sibley's New Mexico Campaign;* Ray C. Colton, *The Civil War in the Western Territories;* and Keleher, *Turmoil in New Mexico,* 143-210. Basic, although now somewhat outdated, is Jack D. Rittenhouse, *New Mexico Civil War Bibliography.*
2. Twitchell, *Military Occupation,* 306. Colonel Loring was accused by Union officers of conspiring with others to convert to the Confederate cause the entire unit of Mounted Rifles (volunteers) then on duty in New Mexico (Keleher, *Turmoil in New Mexico,* 191n).
3. The First Regiment of New Mexico Volunteers had been headed by Ceran St. Vrain until his resignation on September 20, 1861, when Colonel Carson assumed command. Pino's and Chaves' Second Regiment was formally enlisted at Santa Fe during July and August of 1861, for a term of three years. It was probably during that July that Loring tried to woo Manuel to the Southern cause. Chaves himself claimed he spent several weeks of the summer recruiting for the regiment in Socorro and Valencia counties. A story in the *Weekly New Mexico Review* (Santa Fe) for August 16, 1894, says Manuel enlisted every member of his family as a Union volunteer who was old enough to serve. A Third

Regiment was created and placed under Lt. Colonel José M. Valdez. (See E.R.S. Canby to the Adjutant-General of the Army, Fort Craig, March 1, 1862, in *Confederate Victories in the Southwest, From the Official Records,* 138; and Civil War Muster Roll, Descriptive Book, St. Rec. Cen.)

4. Hall, *Sibley's New Mexico Campaign,* 83-103.
5. *Confederate Victories,* 138.
6. These mountains, located in central New Mexico, are not to be confused with the San Mateo Peaks seventy miles farther north and near the village of Cebolleta.
7. This must have been either Francisco Perea, who in 1863 was New Mexico's delegate to Congress, or his uncle, the powerful sheep baron of Bernalillo, José Leandro Perea.
8. Chaves Statement to DeForrest (Compiled Ser. Rec. of Manuel Chaves, R.G. 94, Nat. Arch.).
9. Hall, *Sibley's New Mexico Campaign,* 114.
10. Official Report of Capt. A.S. Thurmond, Sibley's Brigade, Cubero, March 19, 1862 (*Confederate Victories,* 172-73). Thurmond here refers to "Dr. Kavenaugh and his regiment of three men"; obviously the term "regiment" is not being used in an explicit military sense, the same holding for the so-called "regiments" of New Mexico volunteers mentioned frequently in the documents of the period.
11. Theo Noel, in his *A Campaign from Santa Fe to the Mississippi,* indicates that Kavenuagh also maintained a business in Cubero. He says that the doctor "opened his store to us [men of the detachment sent to bring the captured supplies to Albuquerque] and in short notice we were all well clad." (34) On this incident see also Hall, *Sibley's New Mexico Campaign,* 115-16. Had the South won the Civil War, doubtless Kavenaugh would have been remembered as a hero. As it was, as soon as the territory was cleared of Confederate troops, Abraham Cutler, U.S. Marshal for New Mexico, ordered confiscation of the doctor's property (*Rio Abajo Weekly Press,* Albuquerque, January 27, 1863).
12. Hall, *Sibley's New Mexico Campaign,* 119.
13. Chaves Statement to De Forrest (Compiled Ser. Rec. of Manuel Chaves, R.G. 94, Nat. Arch.).
14. Quoted by William Clarke Whitford in his *Colorado Vol-*

unteers in the Civil War. In researching his book, the author interviewed a number of persons, then living, who had participated in the engagement and known Manuel Chaves.

15. Chaves Statement to DeForrest (Compiled Ser. Rec. of Manuel Chaves, R.G. 94, Nat. Arch.) Chivington, who received criticism for not personally leading the attack against the supply train, listed the number of vehicles destroyed at eighty. But Colonel Slough placed it at sixty, a figure in conformity with that of Manuel.
16. Whitford, *Colorado Volunteers*, 122.
17. As reprinted in *Union Army Operations in the Southwest, From the Official Records*, 19-35. A hero in 1862, Chivington later became infamous for his part in the massacre of peaceful Cheyennes at Sand Creek, Colorado, during November of 1864.
18. In addition to Whitford's account cited above, see A.A. Hays, Jr., *New Colorado and the Santa Fe Trail*, 169.
19. Chaves Statement to DeForrest (Compiled Ser. Rec. of Manuel Chaves, R.G. 94, Nat. Arch.).
20. Ibid.
21. Statement of Captain A.W. Evans (Ibid.).
22. Chaves Statement to DeForrest; Paul to Canby, Fort Craig, May 28, 1862; Chaves to Chapin, Santa Fe, June 8, 1862 (Ibid).
23. Chapin to Carson, Santa Fe, May 23, 1862 (Ibid.).
24. Chaves Statement to DeForrest (Ibid.).
25. Undated Report of Capt. A.W. Evans (Ibid.). As a result of his legal difficulties, Manuel had problems collecting the pay owed to him for his military service. On January 24, 1863, he had to apply to General James H. Carleton, Canby's successor, for his back pay. Chaves to Carleton, Peralta (Ibid.).
26. The figure of 30,000 sheep is given by Lummis, *A New Mexico David*, 216. Amado Chaves remembered it as 15,000 (Chaves Ms., Mus. of N.M.), but since Manuel himself claimed a single one of his flocks numbered 11,000, I have accepted Lummis' total as probably the more accurate. Fifty thousand to 100,000 sheep on the larger haciendas was not uncommon in this period.
27. *The Daily New Mexican*, Jan. 22, 1876; and *Index to Congressional Record*, Vol. 15 (Pts. 1-6), 48th Cong., 1st sess., 71.

28. The José María Chaves mentioned here was probably Manuel's brother. Twitchell, in *Spanish Archives of New Mexico*, refers to a brother by this name who married Luz Labadie, the sister of Manuel's wife Vicenta, and was killed by the Navajos (II, 199).
29. Accounts of the battle can be found in Chaves Ms., Mus. of N.M.; Lummis, "A New Mexico Hero," *The Daily New Mexican* (Santa Fe), March 25, 1891; and Twitchell, *Military Occupation*, 307-308. The fight probably occurred in the fall of 1863, not long after Manuel left military service.
30. A recent authoritative study of Carson's campaign against the Navajo is Lawrence Kelly, *Navajo Roundup*.
31. Lorenzo Labadie died at Puerto de Luna on August 10, 1904, at the age of eighty (Keleher, *Turmoil in New Mexico*, 484n).
32. Deed Book H, Santa Fe County Records, 121-22.

Chapter 10: San Mateo

1. Estelle Bennett Burton, "Volunteer Soldiers of New Mexico and Their Conflicts with the Indians in 1862 and 1863," *Old Santa Fe*, 1 (1914), 416.
2. Interview with Floyd Lee, San Mateo, October 12, 1968.
3. June West, "Fernández Ranch," unpublished manuscript in possession of Jack Rittenhouse, Albuquerque.
4. The children, listed in order of their birth, were: Perfilia, Amado, Irineo, Lola, Rosa, Luz, Vicenta, and Manuel (Genealogy, Amado Chaves Col., St. Rec. Cen.).
5. Charles F. Lummis, *A Tramp Across the Continent*, 182-83; and typescript copy of untitled article by Lummis from *The Chillicothe Leader* (Ohio), 1885.
6. Interview with Consuelo Chaves Summers, Santa Fe, November 27, 1968. Mrs. Summers, still living, remembers Comanche Lupe well from her girlhood. Another guest to the Chaves ranch also mentioned the Indian women: "The kitchen was filled with happy and willing servants. I seem to remember especially one, who was called La Cautiva [The Captive], as she had been captured in one of the many raids upon the place and had remained and grown up as a member of the family." (Frances Douglas DeKalb to Erna

Fergusson, Tucson, July 3, 1949. Copy in possession of the author.)

7. This story was related to the author by Floyd Lee of San Mateo, who recalls that Irineo returned to the ranch shortly before his death in 1946 and appeared amazed at the huge size of the trees that he had carried in his suitcase so many years before.
8. Amado Chaves to R.E. Twitchell, Santa Fe, October 19, 1922 (St. Rec. Cen.).
9. Irineo spent time with his elder brother in Washington, where he visited doctors in a futile effort to receive some beneficial treatment for the head injury suffered as a child at Ojuelos (Interview with Consuelo Chaves Summers, Santa Fe, October 22, 1968). Later in life, Irineo became an official interpreter for the Court of Private Land Claims in Santa Fe, and subsequently served with the Rough Riders in the Spanish American War. He died in Albuquerque on February 20, 1946, at the age of ninety (*Santa Fe New Mexican,* February 20, 1946).
10. *The Daily New Mexican* (Santa Fe), April 27, 1876. On May 1, the paper reported that Amado had made a deal with a man named Peters in Georgia to import Angora goats and Merino sheep to New Mexico.
11. Early papers regarding the Fernández Grant can be found in *Report of Private Land Claims in New Mexico,* 43rd Cong., 1st sess., House Ex. Doc. No. 206, 14-19. See also Floyd W. Lee, *Bartolomé Fernández Pioneer Shepherd on the Hills in New Mexico.*
12. *The Daily New Mexican* (Santa Fe), June 20, 1882. In addition to the Fernández and the Cebolleta Grants mentioned, Baca and Chaves also claimed interest in the Cañon de Jémez Grant. Further, Amado was evidently deeply involved in land and mining speculation. Some of his activities and problems are referred to in *The Daily New Mexican* for October 6, 1881; and in Victor Westphall, *The Public Domain in New Mexico, 1854-1891,* 110. That his ventures earned him enemies is suggested by the following brief news item: "Grants, New Mexico. The home of Hon. Amado Chaves was set on fire by incendiaries last night and partly

destroyed. No clue to the parties has yet been found." (*Tombstone Epitaph*, November 19, 1890)

13. Lummis, *A Tramp Across the Continent*, 2. See also a sketch of Lummis' extraordinary life by his principal biographer, Dudley Gordon, "The West's Incomparable Don Carlos," *Harvard Alumni Bulletin*, 69 (1967), 16-23.
14. Typescript of untitled article by Lummis from *The Chillicothe Leader* (Ohio), 1885.
15. Brand Notice in the *Santa Fe New Mexican and Review*, June 6, 1883.
16. Allen E. Erwin, *The Southwest of John H. Slaughter, 1841-1922*, 185. Cahill was shot by the Kid on August 17, 1877.
17. Lummis, *A Tramp Across the Continent*, 183.
18. Ibid., 183-84.
19. Manuel consulted doctors in Albuquerque and Santa Fe, but they provided little relief for his chronically draining leg wounds (Interview with Consuelo Chaves Summers, Santa Fe, October 22, 1968).
20. Lummis, *A New Mexico David*, 217. Rodolfo was the only child of Manuel's eldest daughter Perfilia.
21. *The Daily New Mexican*, August 26, 1885.
22. Amado Chaves was elected speaker of the Territorial Legislature in 1884. In 1891 he became the first Superintendent of Public Instruction, winning acclaim for his efforts to bring educational benefits to remote New Mexican villages. From 1901 to 1903 he served as mayor of Santa Fe. Amado died December 30, 1930 ("Necrology, Amado Chaves," *New Mexico Historical Review*, 6 [1931], 100.) Román Baca served numerous terms in the legislature before his death from diabetes at age sixty-six (*Santa Fe New Mexican*, March 21, 1899).
23. W.G. Ritch (ed.), *New Mexico Blue Book, 1882*, 72.
24. *Santa Fe Daily New Mexican*, February 25, 1883.
25. Lee, *Bartolomé Fernández*, 24.
26. *New Mexican Review-Weekly*, January 31, 1889.
27. Amado Chaves sold the San Mateo ranch in later years, and by the end of World War I, Manuel's chapel was a ruin. About that time, then-owner Floyd Lee decided to tear down the remains of the building, and he summoned

Amado to supervise the removal of his parents' caskets. Inside the log were found two musket balls which Manuel had carried to his grave. Amado also retrieved a gold locket buried with his mother. There is some confusion over what happened to the remains. Lee believes Manuel was taken to the National Cemetery in Santa Fe, where he was entitled to a grave site. But other sources suggest both Manuel and Vicenta were transferred to the local San Mateo cemetery. A search by the author failed to locate the graves at either place.

Bibliography

ARCHIVES AND COLLECTIONS

Museum of New Mexico, History Library, Santa Fe.
Manuel Antonio Chaves File.

National Archives, Washington, D. C.
Compiled Service Record of Manuel Chaves, 1861-1863. Record Group 94.
Department of New Mexico, Letters Received, 1861. Record Group 98.

Santa Fe County Records.
Deed Book A (Registro).

State Records Center and Archives, Santa Fe.
Adjutant General Files:
Miscellaneous Records and Muster Rolls, 1847, 1855, 1862.
Militia Description Book, 1860.
Amado Chaves Collection.
L. Bradford Prince Collection.

University of New Mexico, Special Collections, Albuquerque.
Bureau of Indian Affairs, Superintendency of New Mexico, 1849-1880. Microfilm, Reel 1.
Records of the Office of Indian Affairs, vol. 47, January 21-August 24, 1853. Microfilm, Reel 47.

BOOKS

Abel, A. H., ed. *The Official Correspondence of James S. Calhoun*. Washington, 1915.
Adams, Eleanor B. *Tamaron's Visitation of New Mexico*. Albuquerque, 1954.
Austin, Mary. *Earth Horizon: An Autobiography*. Boston, 1932.
Bandelier, Adolph F. *Report of the United States Commission to the Columbian Historical Expedition at Madrid, 1892-1893*. Washington, 1895.
Barker, Ruth Laughlin. *Caballeros*. New York, 1936.
Calvin, Ross, ed. *Lieutenant Emory Reports*. Albuquerque, 1951.
Cather, Willa. *Death Comes for the Archbishop*. New York, 1955.
Chávez, Fray Angélico. *Origins of New Mexico Familes*. Santa Fe, 1954.
Colton, Ray C. *The Civil War in the Western Territories*. Norman, 1959.
Condition of the Indian Tribes. Washington, 1867.
Confederate Victories in the Southwest, From the Official Records. Albuquerque, 1961.
Cozzens, Samuel Woodworth. *The Marvellous Country*. Boston, 1876.
Cutts, James Madison. *The Conquest of California and New Mexico*. Albuquerque, 1965.
Davis, W. W. H. *El Gringo, Or New Mexico and Her People*. Santa Fe, 1938.
DeVoto, Bernard. *The Year of Decision, 1846*. Boston, 1961.

Dictionary of American Biography. (20 vols.) New York, 1935.

Drumm, Stella M., ed. *Down the Santa Fe Trail and Into Mexico: The Diary of Susan Shelby Magoffin, 1846-1847.* New Haven, 1962.

Emmett, Chris. *Fort Union and the Winning of the Southwest.* Norman, 1965.

Enciclopedia Universal Ilustrada. (70 vols.) Madrid, 1964.

Erwin, Allen E. *The Southwest of John H. Slaughter, 1841-1922.* Glendale, Calif., 1965.

Espinosa, Gilberto and Tibo J. Chaves. *El Rio Abajo.* Belen, N. M., n. d.

Falconer, Thomas. *Letters and Notes on the Texan Santa Fe Expedition, 1841-1842.* New York, 1930.

Frazer, Robert W. *Forts of the West.* Norman, 1965.

Gibson, George Rutledge. *Journal of A Soldier Under Kearny and Doniphan, 1846-1847.* Glendale, Calif., 1935.

Grant, Blanche C. *When Old Trails Were New, The Story of Taos.* New York, 1934.

Gregg, Josiah. *Commerce of the Prairies.* Norman, 1954.

Gulich, Charles Adams, Jr., et. al., eds. *The Papers of Mirabeau Buonaparte Lamar.* (6 vols.) Austin, 1921-28.

Hafen, LeRoy R., ed. *Ruxton of the Rockies.* Norman, 1950.

Hall, Martin Hardwick. *Sibley's New Mexico Campaign.* Austin, 1960.

Hayes, A. A., Jr. *New Colorado and the Santa Fe Trail.* New York, 1880.

Hughes, John T. *Doniphan's Expedition.* Cincinnati, 1848.

Keemle, Charles. *St. Louis Directory for the Years 1838-39.* St. Louis, 1838.

Keleher, William A. *Turmoil in New Mexico, 1846-1868.* Santa Fe, 1952.

Kelly, Lawrence. *Navajo Roundup.* Boulder, 1970.

Kirby, Robert Lee. *The Confederate Invasion of Arizona and New Mexico, 1861-1862.* Los Angeles, 1958.

Lamar, Howard Roberts. *The Far Southwest, 1846-1912.* New Haven, 1966.

Lavender, David. *Bent's Fort*. New York, 1954.
Lee, Floyd W. *Bartolomé Fernández, Pioneer Shepherd on the Hills in New Mexico*. New York, 1954.
Loring, W. W. *A Confederate Soldier in Egypt*. New York, 1884.
Lummis, Charles F. *Mesa, Cañon and Pueblo*. New York, 1925.
——. *A New Mexico David and Other Stories and Sketches of the Southwest*. New Mexico, 1916.
——. *A Tramp Across the Continent*. New York, 1920.
Merk, Frederick. *Manifest Destiny and Mission in American History*. New York, 1966.
Moorhead, Max L. *New Mexico's Royal Road*. Norman, 1958.
Noel, Theo. *A Campaign from Santa Fe to the Mississippi*. Houston, 1961.
Pearce, J. M., ed. *New Mexico Place Names, A Geographical Dictionary*. Albuquerque, 1965.
Ponce de León, José M., ed. *Reseñas Históricas del Estado de Chihuahua*. Chihuahua, 1913.
Read, Benjamín. *Illustrated History of New Mexico*. Santa Fe, 1912.
Ritch, W. G., ed. *New Mexico Blue Book, 1882*. Fac. ed.; Albuquerque, 1968.
Rittenhouse, Jack D. *New Mexico Civil War Bibliography*. Houston, 1961.
Sabin, Edwin L. *Kit Carson Days*. (2 vols.) New York, 1935.
Twitchell, Ralph Emerson. *History of the Military Occupation of New Mexico*. Danville, Ill., 1909.
——. *The Leading Facts of New Mexican History*. (2 vols.) repr. ed.; Albuquerque, 1963.
——. *Old Santa Fe*. New printing; Chicago, 1963.
——. *The Spanish Archives of New Mexico*. (2 vols.) Cedar Rapids, 1914.
Union Army Operations in the Southwest, From the Official Records. Albuquerque, 1961.
Watts, John S. *Indian Depredations in New Mexico*. Washington, 1858.

Westphall, Victor. *The Public Domain in New Mexico, 1854-1891*. Albuquerque, 1965.

Whitford, William Clarke. *Colorado Volunteers in the Civil War*. Denver, 1906.

ARTICLES

Abel, Annie Heloise, ed. "The Journal of John Greiner," *Old Santa Fe*, vol. 3 (1916), 189-243.

Allison, W. W. H., ed. "Santa Fe As It Appeared During the Winter of the Years 1837 and 1838," *Old Santa Fe*, vol. 2 (1914), 170-83.

——. "Santa Fe in 1846," *Old Santa Fe*, vol. 2 (1915) 392-406.

Anonymous. "The Name of Chaves," *El Palacio*, vol. 22 (1927), 112-16.

Bender, A. B. "Frontier Defense in New Mexico, 1853-1861," *New Mexico Historical Review*, vol. 9 (1934), 249-72.

Binkley, William. "New Mexico and the Texan-Santa Fe Expedition," *Southwestern Historical Quarterly*, vol. 28 (1923), 85-107.

Bloom, Lansing B. "Necrology, Amado Chaves," *New Mexico Historical Review*, vol. 6 (1931), 101-04.

——. "New Mexico Under Mexican Administration, 1822-1846," *Old Santa Fe*, vol. 1 (1914), 235-87.

Briggs, Walter. "The Lady They Called Tules," *New Mexico Magazine*, vol. 49 (1971), 9-16.

Burton, Estelle Bennett. "Volunteer Soldiers of New Mexico and Their Conflicts with the Indians in 1862 and 1863," *Old Santa Fe*, vol. 1 (1914), 386-419.

Chávez, Fray Angélico. "Doña Tules, Her Fame and Her Funeral," *El Palacio*, vol. 57 (1950), 227-34.

——. "Don Fernando Durán de Chávez," *El Palacio*, vol. 55 (1948), 105-07.

——. "José González, Genízaro Governor," *New Mexico Historical Review*, vol. 30 (1955), 190-94.

Gordon, Dudley. "The West's Incomparable Don Carlos," *Harvard Alumni Bulletin*, vol. 69 (1967), 16-23.

Heyman, Max L., Jr. "On the Navajo Trail: The Campaign of 1860-61," *New Mexico Historical Review*, vol. 26 (1951), 44-63.

Hodge, F. W., ed. "Combs Narrative of the Santa Fe Expedition in 1841," *New Mexico Historical Review*, vol. 5 (1930), 305-14.

Marino, C. C. "The Seboyetans and the Navajos," *New Mexico Historical Review*, vol. 29 (1954), 8-27.

Mauzy, Wayne L. "Recollections of Demetrio Pérez: The Old Palace in Mexican Days," *El Palacio*, vol. 67 (1967), 87-94.

Reeve, Frank D. "The Federal Indian Policy in New Mexico, 1858-1880," *New Mexico Historical Review*, vol. 12 (1937), 218-69.

Reno, Phillip. "Rebellion in New Mexico—1837," *New Mexico Historical Review*, vol. 40 (1965), 197-213.

Simmons, Marc. "Horse Race at Fort Fauntleroy, An Incident of the Navajo Wars," *La Gaceta* of the Santa Fe Corral of the Westerners, vol. 5 (1970), 3-13.

Smith, George Winston and Charles Judah, eds. "Manifest Destiny: War in the West," *New Mexico Quarterly*, vol. 38 (1968), 44-64.

Taylor, Morris F. "Action at Fort Massachusetts: The Indian Campaign of 1855," *Colorado Magazine*, vol. 42 (1965), 292-310.

——. "Campaigns Against the Jicarilla Apache, 1855," *New Mexico Historical Review*, vol. 45 (1970), 269-91.

Tyler, Daniel. "Gringo Views of Manuel Armijo," *New Mexico Historical Review*, vol. 45 (1970), 23-46.

Winfrey, Dorman A. "Mirabeau B. Lamar and Texas Nationalism," *Southwestern Historical Quarterly*, vol. 59 (1955), 176-90.

Unpublished Studies

Carter, Allen A. "The Legend of Tomé." Ms. in files of New Mexico Writer's Project, Museum of New Mexico, Santa Fe.

Minge, Ward Alan. "Frontier Problems in New Mexico Preceding the Mexican War, 1840-1846." Ph. D. dissertation, 1965, University of New Mexico, Albuquerque.

Newspapers

The Chillicothe Leader (Ohio).
1885.

New Mexican Review-Weekly, Santa Fe.
Jan. 31, 1889.

Rio Abajo Weekly Press, Albuquerque.
Jan. 27, 1863.

Santa Fe Daily New Mexican.
Jan. 22, 1876; Apr. 27, 1876; June 20, 1882; Feb. 25, 1883; June 6, 1883; Mar. 25, 1891; Jan. 28, 1893; Mar. 21, 1899; Aug. 11, 1904; and Feb. 20, 1946.

Santa Fe Weekly Gazette.
Oct. 31, 1857.

St. Louis Daily Globe-Democrat.
Aug. 15, 1888.

Tombstone Epitaph (Arizona).
Nov. 19, 1890.

Acknowledgments

In composing this biography of Manuel Chaves, I incurred many debts. Consuelo Chaves Summers, last living grandchild of Manuel, gave access to the papers of her late father, Amado Chaves, recounted important bits of family history, and encouraged advancement of the project. Her son, Amado Chaves Summers, as devoted a horseman as was his great-grandfather, permitted copies to be made of portraits of Manuel and his beautiful wife Vicenta.

J.K. Shiskin deserves my special thanks for digging out numerous references I otherwise would have missed. Susie Henderson, former librarian of the Museum of New Mexico, also provided many useful leads. Fray Angélico Chávez graciously took time from his ecclesiastical labors to answer my questions regarding the genealogy of his family and extended permission for use of the Chaves escutcheon that appeared originally in his *Origins of New Mexico Families*.

George Clayton Pearl and Boleslo Romero of Tomé guided me to the site of the Chaves hacienda at Ojuelos, while

William A. Goff helped clarify certain points regarding Manuel's brief career in Missouri. J. Lee Correll of Navajo Parks and Recreation, Window Rock, Arizona, kindly furnished copies of materials he discovered in the National Archives concerning Manuel Chaves' part in the tragic horse race at Fort Fauntleroy. To Floyd Lee of San Mateo, I owe thanks for several stories about Manuel's later career. Also I must acknowledge the help of Dr. Myra Ellen Jenkins of the New Mexico State Records Center and Archives, Dr. Jack Wilson, Professor David Weber, Dr. Dudley Gordon, Dr. Peggy Ladenberger, and Archie West, owner of Old Green. Lili West read the entire manuscript and offered helpful suggestions for its improvement.

Finally I wish to recognize the encouragement and support of blacksmiths Frank Turley and Skip Rowe, good "pards" both. They'll do to ride the river with.

M.S.

Index

Italic numerals indicate photos.